A unique collection of examples of God reaching out to us with his love and comfort. We are promised God's help, and for many of us this has come in the form of angels.

Pastor Don McCall

Although we believe the Bible to be God's Word and true, I wonder if we assign angels more to the realm of nice stories and fairy tales. This compilation of experiences shows angels to be very real, present and relational. God uses them to show his love for us and to bring us closer to him. May you be blessed and encouraged as you read these stories, as I have been.

Jo Smith

What an amazing witness to God's interaction with us! It speaks volumes to the fact and reality that God is present here and now.

Pastor Dirk Willner

Angels are Here

Over 80 true stories of angels,
visions
and other personal encounters with God

Compiled by **Joyleen Edwards**

Copyright © 2021 Joyleen Edwards

Angels are Here
Compiled by Joyleen Edwards

ISBN 978-0-646-83693-5

Unless otherwise indicated, Scripture quotations are taken from the New Revised Standard Version (NRSV). Copyright © 1989 National Council of the Churches of Christ in the United States of America. Used with permission. All rights reserved worldwide.

Scripture quotations marked NIV are taken from the New International Version. Copyright © 1973, 1978, 1984 by International Bible Society. Used with permission of Zondervan. All rights reserved worldwide.

Scripture quotations marked NCV are taken from the New Century Version. Copyright © 2005 by Thomas Nelson. Used with permission. All rights reserved.

Scripture quotations marked ESV are taken from the English Standard Version. Copyright © 2001 by Crossway, a publishing ministry of Good News Publishers. Used with permission. All rights reserved.

All royalties donated to Australian Lutheran World Service for clean water projects in developing countries.

Dedicated to my mother,
Edna Vonow,
whose angel and vision stories
made her voice sparkle in the telling.

Contents

Part 1: Angels

The Voice in the Night, *Joyleen Edwards* 21
Rescued by an Angel, *Fiona Muller* 23
Angelic Encounters, *Cindy Kloeden* 26
The Bright Figure, *Pastor Brian Keller* 31
Angelic Guidance, *Penny Vine* 35
Angels in Action, *Robyn Wuttke* 36
Angels on the Ceiling, *Wayne Muller* 40
Hello, *Edna Vonow* 42
Perfect Timing, *Margaret Ward* 42
Angels as a Sign, *Name withheld* 43
Calling My Name, *Catherine Boreham* 45
Angel in Full Armour, *Darren Booth* 46
Chatting with Angels, *Pastor Dirk Willner* 47
Entertaining Angels Unawares, *R & M Brown* 51
Today I Saw an Angel, *Rick Jenkins* 53
Mack's Angel, *Rick Jenkins* 55
Miraculous Rescue, *Myrna Frohling* 57
Money for the Meter, *Mandee Anderson* 59
My Guardian Angel, *Meagan Edwards* 61
Tapping on My Shoulder, *Edna Vonow* 63
Our Angel Protectors, *Pr Graeme van Brummelen* 64
My Two Angel Protectors, *Robin Jaensch* 67
Not Yet His Time, *Edna Randall* 70
Rescue in the City, *Wendy Millan* 72
Saved from Drowning, *Robert Brown* 75
The Angel Choir, *Lois Salzke* 77
He Kept Me Awake, *Colin Letchford* 78
The Trumpeting Angel, *Darren Booth* 80
The Boy with the Glow, *Geoff Severin* 81

Almost Certain Death, *Robert Mills* 85
The Gowned Figure, *Colin Letchford* 87
The Guards, *Name withheld* 88
The Smiling Angel, *Kathy Wendt* 89
The Rescue, *Di McClelland* 92
Two White Figures, *Hilary Park* 93
Journeying with My Angel, *Brad Nielsen* 95
Angel in the Mirror, *Rachel Bichel* 104
Stairway to Heaven, *Bev Schumacher* 106
On Guard, *Vanessa Thompson* 107
Christ in Sight, *Amelia* 109
Portals in my Classroom, *Ethan* 110

Part 2: Visions
God's Handwriting, *Kayleen Proctor* 115
The Blue Van, *Pastor Rob Edwards* 118
Transformation, *Asau Da Costa* 120
Armour of God, *Helen Vonow* 123
Freedom for Samantha, *June Wicks* 125
I Saw God, *Maaret Sinkko* 126
At Perfect Peace, *Kingsley Vonow* 127
Guidance for Our Mission, *Anabel de Souza Lima* 129
Direction for My Future, *Pastor Rob Edwards* 130
My Mother in Heaven, *Edna Vonow* 132
My Husband in Heaven, *Edna Vonow* 133
Encircling Angels, *Edna Vonow* 134
Jesus Comes to Visit, *Sibylle Walker* 135
An Immediate Answer, *Ruth Eames* 136
Living the Dream, *Evilasio Oliveira* 137
Meeting Jesus, *Rev Anneli Sinkko* 139
My Daughter in Heaven, *Lesley Bain* 141
God Spoke to Me, *Abelita Espirito Santo* 144
Two Big Arms, *Abelita Espirito Santo* 145

The Comforter, *Margaret Ward* 146
The Bright Light, *Margaret Ward* 147
Seeing Jesus at Communion, *Margaret Ward* 148
The Door, *Win Perry* 149
The Pine Box, *Lynne Newbold* 151
The Reality of God, *Ian Pertzel* 153
You are too Early, *Lois Salzke* 155

Part 3: Hearing God's Voice, and More
Serve My People Well, *Lee-Anne Kupke* 159
A Disaster Averted, *Janette Heintze* 160
A Life-Saving Nudge, *Name withheld* 162
A Word of Comfort, *Name withheld* 162
A Precious Touch, *Robyn Wuttke* 163
A Strange Sensation, *Name withheld* 165
My Father's Transformation, *Lois Dunchue* 166
One Last Goodbye, *Don McCall* 169
Pinned to the Ground, *Pastor Rodney Witmitz* 173
The Returning Cows, *Hollie Joyce* 175
The Foot, *Name withheld* 177
The Unknown Woman, *Name withheld* 177
The Gift of Extra Time, *Margot Durow* 178
The Healing of the Sheep, *Andrew Vonow* 179
The Strong Hand, *Norelle Behrendorff* 181
The White Dove, *Margaret Ward* 183
The Power on My Back, *Edna Randall* 184
The God of Miracles, *Joselyn Khan* 185
The Aura, *Edna Vonow* 189
Jesus Loves Me, *Merrelyn Zanker* 190

Preface

The collection of these stories began following a conversation with my mother regarding a number of supernatural experiences she'd had during her life. As she spoke, it soon became evident that something extremely special and reverent was being shared. The angels and visions that came were inextricably linked to her current life happenings. The timing was always perfect, and the peace, like no other. As such, I felt compelled to record them.

Once recorded, I became curious as to just how many more untold stories were out there. To my surprise, they were everywhere! It didn't seem to matter who I was talking to (or where I was), either that person had experienced something themselves, or they knew of someone else who had. It was really exciting, and I knew I wanted to share those stories with as many people as possible.

Introduction

The purpose of this book is to present to you stories showing the real presence of God in the lives of ordinary people. It is to demonstrate that because God is a creative God, he is able to come to us in whatever way he chooses—through the sending of angels, through visions, through the hearing of his audible voice; whatever …

The stories within are not fictitious. They come from family, friends and acquaintances—men, women and children. For many, it will be the first time they will have made their story known. While for privacy reasons some people's names have been withheld, it does not make their story any less legitimate.

What you make of these stories is up to you, but I believe there are too many, and they hold way too much value for them to be mere figments of over-active imaginations. It is my hope that in reading them you will be encouraged, and perhaps even a little challenged, as to the reality of God, and heaven, and the purpose behind such experiences.

Verses from the Bible have been added so that you may see how people's experiences have the backing of God's Word.

It is my great pleasure to present these stories to you, and deep appreciation goes to the 66 people who contributed so willingly and voluntarily in order to help others come to know of the reality of a caring, intervening God.

Part 1

Angels

Have you ever wondered about the many little coincidences of life, like being in exactly the right place, at the right time, for the right outcome to occur? Have you ever been so overcome with a sense of peace it was as though your guardian angel was right there with you? Have you ever had one of those 'close shaves' whilst driving, after which you think, *There had to be someone looking out for me there?*

I'm sure we can never imagine the number of times and places where angels, through the will of God, have kept us safe from harm and directed us to him!

What are Angels and What do They Look Like?

Angels are God's messengers, and they carry out the tasks he gives them. They help us out in our time of need and point us to God. Sometimes we have the privilege of seeing them, but because they are spiritual beings, it is not necessarily so (Colossians 1:16). When we do see them, their appearance can vary from as much as being dazzling white (Matthew 28:2-4), to looking like real people (Hebrews 13:2). In the Bible, angels always appear as fully grown adults, usually men. It seems that some have wings, but this is not always the case.

What is the Purpose of Angels?

The primary purpose of angels is to serve God. They do this by worshipping and praising him (Isaiah 6:1-3), communicating his will to people and providing them with guidance (Acts 8:26), providing for people's physical needs (Genesis 21:17-20), protecting and/or delivering people from danger (Daniel 3 and 6), bringing strength, encouragement and peace to those in need (Acts 5:19-20), answering prayer (Daniel 9:20-24 and 10:10-12), and comforting the dying by bringing peace and hope (Luke 16:22). [1]

Linda Stover has this delightful description–

> *"Angels are the essence of love and joy, they are created to love and serve without condition, they are the guardians of our souls, they are a bundle of God's ever-present love and grace, they communicate through thoughts, music and the environment, and they are created to serve, love, hold and support those to whom they are assigned."* [2]

And Mary C. Neal, in her fascinating book *To Heaven and Back*, written following her near-death experience in which she communicated with angels, has this to say–

> *"Although we are rarely aware of angels or their intervention in our world, I believe there are angels all around us every day of our lives. Angels are spirit beings who are mentioned more than 250 times in both the Old Testament and the New Testament in the Bible. They appear as creatures, events, and humans,*

offering praise and worship to God. They care for, protect, and guide God's people, frequently intervening or bringing messages to people from God. They are the ones orchestrating the 'coincidences' that occur so commonly in our lives."
[3]

The Voice in the Night

Joyleen Edwards

I shall begin with my own story.

It was January 2010 and I was in Phuket holidaying with my daughter and her two female friends. I had been enjoying the sights and sounds of the place very much, but at the same time couldn't seem to shake a sense of heaviness that lingered in and around me. I didn't know where it came from, but it seemed linked to the strong Buddhist influence there–especially the worship of idols. As a Christian I did not feel threatened by this, but it did leave me feeling perturbed.

Something then happened which brought me the very peace I needed. It was the middle of the third night and I believe I was visited either by an angel, or by God himself. I was fast asleep in a double-bed I was sharing with my daughter, when as clear as a bell I heard a strong male voice say to me, not once, but three times, "You have been baptised into the blood of Jesus Christ." At this, I instantly sat up and put on the light to see who was there. The only person was my daughter ... certainly no male! The voice did not frighten me. It did not seem strange. It just felt comforting and reassuring.

Some time later as I was reading the Bible, I came across this in Romans 6:3, *"Do you not know that all of us who have been baptised into Christ Jesus were baptised into his death?"* To me this confirmed that the voice was from God—either directly, or via one of his angels. I believe that in speaking to me in such a way, God was assuring me that even in a Buddhist country I was still firmly his, and that because of my baptism (which, incidentally, took place when I was a baby), nothing could take that away from me.

This first-time-ever event well and truly cured me of my scepticism that such a thing could happen, and solidly affirmed his very real presence in my life. It is something I shall never forget.

Based on this, I came to see that if God could come to me in this way, then surely he could come to other people in whatever way he chose as well, in order to meet *their* needs. He could send actual angels, he could send angels in the form of people, he could speak through visions ... he could do whatever he liked! I am now no longer surprised to hear of the variety of ways people say God has come to them and helped them—and of the perfect timing in which they have always occurred.

Rescued by an Angel

Fiona Muller

Our fourth child, Vashti, was born on the 14th March 2001. Life was hectic. Not only were there four children under the age of five to care for, but I was also helping to run our family property as well as being actively involved in church and community work.

The drought years had begun and the temperature was still quite warm for that time of year. I was sitting outside under our back verandah breastfeeding Vashti, the new baby I had just brought home from the hospital. My mother, Ruth, was also there, and we were chatting away while watching the other kids play.

When the workmen turned up to work on a building project, I decided to go back into the house to finish feeding Vashti. Ruth and I would have only been inside for about fifteen minutes when two completely wet and muddy children (Rachael four, and Tyson two) walked in.

As a mother I instantly thought the worst, as we have a very large, deep dam alongside our home for garden and stock water. A wave of panic came over me. Even though my children were safe, I could not help thinking about what could so easily have been. It took me over an hour to calm down and actually hear what they were trying to explain about what had happened to them.

In her simple child language, this is what Rachael said–

"Mummy, a big white ghosta with big wings and a big sword told us to get out of the dam and go back home. He was very big and helped us get out of the water." This she repeated over and over again. It seemed she needed to do this so that I would actually stop and listen to the amazing miracle that had just occurred.

My husband and I believe that either Jesus, or an angel, were there that day with our children. I got Rachael to draw a picture of what she had seen, and it continues to hang framed in her room as a reminder of the fact that God's protection is very real in our lives today.

Now while you may be tempted to think that one of the workmen must have rescued our children, we know that was not possible as they were on the top of the cottage roof that was being built at the time. Their father, Neil, and Greg, were in the machinery shed. Nobody took any notice of the children wandering off. The picture that Rachael drew does not show builders. If the builders had pulled her and her brother from the dam, I'm sure they would have let us know that it was them. Also, when we questioned the builders later on, they had no idea of the incident.

I believe it is so easy (especially as adults) to shut out the supernatural realm and operate from an earthly perspective, but we as a family have experienced so many more supernatural incidents since Rachael's angel experience that we have no doubt that God is real and active. We are always excited to see the amazing things he does in the lives of people around us.

*For he will command his angels concerning
you to guard you in all your ways.*

Psalm 91:11

Angelic Encounters

Cindy Kloeden

During the early stages of planning for Edgar Mayer's 'Surprised by the Holy Spirit' Conference held here in Victor Harbour in August 2014, I was working with some part of the plans when I was interrupted by the Holy Spirit.

I was given a vision where I 'saw' with my spiritual eyes, a map of South Australia. It was as though I was above the state of SA– I could see the borders of our state and the land just beyond the borders. Then I saw *him*, the precious Holy Spirit, circling and soaring above South Australia (part of the 'Great Southland of the Holy Spirit').

The purpose of his presence was to call and gather those he wanted to be present at the conference where he would be honoured and spoken of. And there he remained, right up till the conference days, soaring over our state calling and gathering. From the vision, I knew, with a knowing outside of my own ability, that this was a meeting that was bigger than Victor Harbour Lutheran Church, this city, and the surrounding areas.

In continuing the planning, I asked our Father for the number we would host for the conference, and was given 320. I don't know the final figure, but registrations were over 300–and this did not include those who came for Friday evening only, and those who served us through hospitality.

Back to the topic of 'Angelic Encounters' ... Saturday of the conference our planning seemed to go out the window, as the morning tea slot slipped away and we headed towards the lunchtime slot–not my planning, but the Heavenly Host was doing a work in the spiritual–a work I didn't see until I asked him to show me what was going on. And he did. Again, with spiritual eyesight, I saw huge angels in our worship space carrying out chains that had been broken from the people within the room. They were carrying them out through the aisles between the seating. That was a pretty awesome sight–seeing God's work of releasing people, and his angelic army carrying out his work. I slipped from my chair, made my way to Tatjana Mayer, Pastor Edgar's wife, and told her what I had seen. I then returned to my seat (the plan was to report to her if we saw or heard anything from God). I thought no more of this till near the end of Saturday night's session.

Saturday evening was a time for prayer. Prayer opportunities were made available at various times during the conference, and as the major part of the day was over, I could relax a little, and marvel at what God was doing, and had done so far. I approached Helen, the chief intercessor from Living Grace Church Toowoomba (of which Edgar is the pastor), to pray for me. Her first words to me were ones that confirmed the earlier work of the angels carrying out chains, saying that what I had seen was what she and others had also seen in the spiritual realm. Her words encouraged me. People attending the conference were encouraged to come for prayer as many times as they chose, and to whomever they chose–the prayer team being a combination of people from our church, Toowoomba, and elsewhere. I received prayer from Pastor Edgar Mayer late Saturday evening.

Following the prayer time, as I was spending time with the Lord, I was aware of two angels kneeling on either side of me. With spiritual eyesight I watched as they 'attended to me', making some alterations to my clothing–a military jacket that I was wearing in the spiritual realm. They were changing the status of the epaulettes on my shoulders by placing new ones on, as well as changing each button down the jacket's front. The angels were larger than cherubim size, but not the size of the huge ones I had seen earlier. They were angels that had different tasks to carry out. This was a most enjoyable and amazing experience.

What I was to hear a couple of weeks later, told me by a young Lutheran man who was attending the conference (and who, unbeknownst to me, was assisting Edgar at the time I received prayer and the angels were altering my clothing), really amazed me:

"I heard that a three-year-old child said to her mother, 'Mummy, look at the beautiful ladies with that lady over there!' "The lady this little girl was pointing to was you, and the 'beautiful ladies', the angels." The man went on to tell me that at that point I was there alone, that is, there were no other people immediately around me. The little child's heart and eyes were open to be able to see beyond the physical realm.

When I heard this story, I was amazed, excited and encouraged ...

but this man had even more to tell that was just as amazing and encouraging. During Saturday afternoon of the conference, as I was sitting on a stool on the eastern side of the worship space interceding for someone in need, this young man had looked over, seen me, and said to himself, "That's one of the people who organised this conference–and she's praying ... no, she's interceding." Then he told me how he had seen two large angels dressed in armour, one standing on either side of me, standing guard. Wow! I had not been aware of them.

I am wondering how much we miss because we aren't aware of what is happening around us, our Father taking care of us, his angelic army about his business ... I wonder just how many more stories there were that weekend, or the following weekend, or any time really, that we are not aware of that would encourage others?

Whether you believe my story or not doesn't matter to me. It is my story; my testimony. Scripture is full of angelic encounters and dreams, visions and holy trances, and God is still speaking to us today.

Are not all angels ministering spirits sent to serve those who will inherit salvation?

Hebrews 1:14 NIV

*In the last days, God says,
I will pour out my Spirit on all people.
Your sons and daughters will prophesy,
your young men will see visions,
your old men will dream dreams.
Even on my servants, both men and women,
I will pour out my Spirit in those days,
and they will prophesy.*

Acts 2:17-18 NIV

The Bright Figure

Pastor Brian Keller

"You should be a pastor!" Those were the thoughtful words of a well-respected member of my home congregation at Pella, Victoria. It was December 1965.

Maybe the seed had been sown, but it had certainly lay dormant for many years as far as I was concerned. Then early in our married life, probably around 1976, I said to my wife, Elaine, "I'm thinking of studying to become a pastor."

Her reaction was swift and not very encouraging–"I don't think you would be a very good pastor," or words to that effect.

Well that seemed quite definite, so on I kept with farming activities around Goolgowi, New South Wales. Only much later did Elaine reveal to me that what she really meant was that she wasn't ready for such a huge step in life–and looking back I can see that we were both lacking in maturity in life experiences, and in our faith journeys. It is interesting that the spark was really fanned into flame when we attended a weekend seminar at Bathurst on the topic of 'Worship', led by Dr John Kleinig from Luther Seminary in Adelaide.

Some years later I again raised the topic, and this time the reaction was much more positive. The whole process of discussing the matter with our district president, filling in the application forms, and the interview at Luther Seminary, all went extremely smoothly. We sold our home in Griffith in two weeks at a time when properties were not selling, a congregation member offered to move our possessions to Adelaide in his farm truck, we had a choice of units to move into in Adelaide, and Elaine was offered a job. It seemed that God had all this planned out for us and we were simply being obedient.

But let's go back a few months. While it appeared to be very straightforward with everything falling into place, there was a continual battle going on in my head and heart. Night after night I would lie awake asking myself and asking God, "Am I doing the right thing? Is this what you want me to do? I need a sign. Any sign! You can scratch an answer into the gyprock wall—we can repair it. Maybe an angel, or even Jesus himself, could come down and say or do something." Night after night, prayer after prayer. While the congregation members gave great encouragement and assistance, what I needed was some sign; some affirmation from heaven.

Study at Luther Seminary began in 1985. What a challenge! I was in the largest class ever to start a year and I found study difficult and time-consuming. It wasn't my natural disposition to be sitting around reading, writing, listening to lectures and facing exams. I think I can say it was by grace that I continued to succeed and to move forward onto each new challenge.

Field-work was part of our training. I decided to go beyond the usual congregations on the Adelaide Plains up into the hills at Blackwood. Here the congregation welcomed my involvement in various areas of service, even to being included in a Christmas musical. Sunday School and Youth were fun but then a small group of young university students from the congregation asked me to lead studies on a regular basis. That frightened me. I already knew these young people, and they challenged everything–sometimes even just for fun, although I wasn't to know that till later.

I'm uncertain if it was the first, or second, or even the third study night with this group, but I was starting to feel quite out of my depth with their questions and discussion. My biblical knowledge, my Lutheran understanding of 'church', my knowledge of various ethical issues, my understanding of our culture, was on a huge learning curve. It still is. Anyway, on this one particular night as we were travelling home along Portrush Road, and within a few hundred metres of our townhouse in Payneham, I said to Elaine, "It's all too hard. I can't do it. I'm going to leave the seminary." At this, she nearly fell out of the car, even though the doors were locked! But I was certain. If this was what the pastor was expected to do, then I couldn't do it. The feeling was very strong.

The time must have been nearing midnight. Lying in bed I wrestled with my thoughts and what I had shared with Elaine. In prayer, I struggled to let God know how I felt, and I wanted some response. If being a pastor was what God wanted me to do, then I needed help.

As I dozed off, something beautiful, yet strange, happened. At the foot of our bed was a figure in bright white. Was it an angel? Was it Jesus himself? I have always believed it was Jesus. That was my immediate reaction. But I am happy to say it was an angel if that is correct. I'm not going to argue with God on that point. The room was filled with peace, and I had no fear. The message spoken was simple–"It's going to be alright." And then it was over. This was the sign I had been waiting for!

The experience was real, but my first reaction was to check the entire unit to make sure no other human was present. Yes, the windows and doors were locked. There was no one in the wardrobe! And then I had the best sleep.

In the morning I told Elaine what had happened. She hadn't seen anything, but sensed that something special had occurred. That night was a turning point, and encouragement, and a very special gift from God that enabled me to complete my studies, and to serve as a pastor for more than 20 years. It was also the beginning of other experiences where God has revealed his Spirit in various ways–but that is for another time.

In the Bible, Matthew described his encounter with an angel of the Lord this way - *"His appearance was like lightning, and his clothing white as snow."* (Matthew 28:3)

Angelic Guidance

Penny Vine

A single parent who had worked hard to escape a violent marriage, and had one child (a 21-year-old who had recently been diagnosed with leukaemia and was commencing chemotherapy), was in Sydney to see the renal consultant.

While there she learned that she needed to have an urgent operation, but feeling as though all her energy should be going into caring for her son, not being in hospital meeting her own needs, pleaded some time to consider it. From a medical perspective, if she didn't have the operation now it would be a much more difficult procedure in the future.

Sitting at Redfern Station on her journey to the airport, she was agonising about the difficult decision she was facing when suddenly she sensed a loving presence; an awareness of a person of light beside her.

At the same time, she experienced a loud but loving voice in her head telling her to go ahead with the operation and that all would be well for both her and her son. The sense of peace stayed with her throughout the time ahead as she proceeded with the operation–and her son recovered fully from his leukaemia.

Angels in Action

Robyn Wuttke

I thought it was very appropriate to start sharing my story today (9th August 2011) as it was one year ago that my mother died and the story, with its two special parts, actually happened.

I had come over to Henty in New South Wales from my home in South Australia to spend a few days with Mum, so I could help her and Dad in and out of the hospital. She was much sicker that we all thought. In the morning we had been phoned into the hospital by the night nurses, as Mum was breathing heavily. I was supposed to be catching the plane back to Adelaide at 9am from Albury. My bags were packed so Dad and I headed into the hospital along with the rest of the family from Henty. We thought I would stay for a while and then my brother would drop me into Albury.

Mum was not well. We were all crying and singing hymns of praise around her. I knew I couldn't catch the plane now but it was tricky to know what to do. I phoned my husband in Adelaide and said, "I can't go now. Mum is not well. What should I do?"

He said, "We'll pray." I hopped off the phone, praying.

Only minutes later Adrian rang back and said, "You would never believe it! The airline's just phoned to say that your flight has been postponed for eight hours due to maintenance needed on the plane."

I hopped off the phone and told my family. We all rejoiced. My brother, Neil, laughed as he told us how he had seen two big angels watching over Mum last night, saying how they must have gone for a slight diversion and tinkered with my plane a little!

We prayed, cried and continued to sing around Mum's bed telling her often how much we loved her. The youngest granddaughter, Esther, was sitting on her dad's knee near Grandma. She was intently looking up at the ceiling, eyes focussed on something important.

My brother Wayne said, "We've seen this look before. She's seeing angels." Shortly after, Mum died. We all have no doubt she *was* seeing angels.

I hung out with the family for the day after Mum died, which was so precious. Eight hours later Dad took me to the airport, and we hugged lots, knowing that the next time we would be seeing each other would be at the funeral. As I was sitting getting ready to board the plane, I listened to lots of the passengers discussing the cancellation.

"The plane never gets cancelled for eight hours–maybe for a few hours, but never this long!" I couldn't help but tell those near me about my mum, and that God had done something special today for me with the plane cancellation. This certainly quietened the conversation down! This was the first amazing thing that happened.

Now for the second. I boarded the plane soon after, heading to

Sydney before catching the connecting flight to Adelaide. I made it to Sydney alright, but there was barely enough time for me to make my next flight. Adrian had told me it would be tight. I hopped off the plane as quickly as I could and tried to find my boarding gate. I could hear my name being called over the speaker system. I was very late. I asked at a station for my boarding gate and I had a long way to run. I ran fast and eventually got to my gate.

"Are you Robyn?" they asked.

"Yes," I said.

A young guy in a high viz jacket then said, "I'll take her to the plane."

I followed him down the gangway. On the way he asked me about my day. I told him about my mum dying and the miracles that had happened, and how lucky it was that I was holding things together or I would be crying all over his shoulder. He was such an encouragement to me in his words and manner. We got to the plane and he said, "She's here now," and then almost instantly was gone. He was nowhere to be seen.

I searched for my seat then and found I was sitting between two men. It had been a big day, and I was very close to tears. Just as I was trying to get settled and not cry, the hostesses came down the aisle and said, "Robyn, come with us."

Oh no, I thought. *Now I am in trouble*!

"We hear you have had a hard day."

They took me down to the front of the plane and sat me in

business class. They got me a cup of tea, a box of tissues and looked after my bag. I cried lots as the plane took off. They were so kind to me. Halfway through the flight I asked them how they knew about my day, and if my husband had rung the airlines. They said, "No, that guy you were with … he told us!"

I can't explain it, but I know in my heart, and truly believe, that the man in the high-viz shirt was an angel sent by God to bring blessing and comfort (something I especially felt later as I was relaying this story to my brothers and family).

God is *so* good!

Angels on the Ceiling

Wayne Muller

This relates to the previous story.

In August 2011 my sister, my brother with his family, and me with my family, were called to the hospital where my mother who had been sick, was passing away. We gathered around her bedside and although my mum was not conscious, we knew she was still able to understand us being there.

My brother and I have five children each, and so together with the ten children who were present, we had a wonderful time of each sharing what we loved about Mum (Grandma), the things that made us laugh and how much we loved her. We all then had the chance to pray with her, and sing the songs about Jesus to her that she had taught us.

We were gathered around her–I was sitting by her bed and my sister was sitting next to me. My two-year-old daughter, Esther, was lying on my lap staring up at the ceiling. As she was doing so, it became obvious that her eyes were following something moving. I pointed this out to my sister and shared with her how I believed Esther was seeing angels.

It was at that very moment that my sister touched me and pointed to Mum. Her breathing had stopped. Suddenly there was this overwhelming sense that little Esther had seen the angels taking my mum to Jesus and up into heaven. It was an experience of sensing heaven's doors opening, and we all felt the atmosphere of heaven among us.

We all know, but especially Esther, that Grandma is with Jesus in heaven. It was an experience and a day we will never forget.

Hello

Edna Vonow

A month ago in my sleep I was gently disturbed by an angel standing beside my bed. He appeared in a shimmering blue and silver mist, and wore a long white gown. On his head was a beautiful floral wreath. I said "Hello" to him, and he said "Hello" back. Following that, he promptly disappeared. I believe that God is using such experiences as this to continually encourage me to be his child and to strengthen my faith.

Perfect Timing

Margaret Ward

One day when my friend, Merleen, and her mum were shopping in Bayliss Street, Wagga Wagga, New South Wales, Merleen's mum fell right in the path of an oncoming truck as she was crossing the road. What would normally have ended up in certain death, however, didn't. As the truck approached, Merleen's mum saw and felt an angel hurriedly roll her to the centre of the road out of the truck's way. She escaped unharmed.

Angels as a Sign

Name withheld

In the evenings, I like to take our dog for a walk. It's a time for him to check out the remnants of the day's activities and for me a chance to see curlews, marvel at the night skies (I especially like to track the constellation of Scorpio and the planet Jupiter), and have time out with my God. On these walks I tend to bring more problems than thanks to Jesus. Sometimes my heart is full of anguish, and the depths are in equal measure to the happiness.

Years ago, when my marriage started to see-saw as an 'unspoken crisis', I lamented to God, and he said quite plainly, "Your marriage is dead." He told me what was wrong and it was just what I needed to hear. It was a breath of fresh air.

As I approached our home on the way back from my walk that one night, I said to God, "If you want me to stay with Graham (not his real name), I will stay. If you want me to go, I will go." It was at that point I felt an angel stand on either side of me. Each was very powerful and tall. I could not look around or to the side because I was terrified. God's presence was everywhere and it was very heavy upon me.

After this, the angels left, but God was still there. I went inside the house and my husband said, "Are you alright?" I told him I was fine.

He said, "Are you sure? You are as white as a ghost! You are very pale. Go and check yourself out."

I openly confess Jesus Christ as my Lord and Saviour. I pray for my family continually, and I especially ask that my husband's heart will be opened to receive Jesus. Jesus has been very patient with me, and he is asking me to be patient and kind to my husband. God has shown me his grace in this sign of the angels and I know I will be protected when I do work in his holy name.

Calling My Name

Catherine Boreham

My trust is in the Lord Jesus Christ, and he is my strength and shield. Quite a few years ago, the Lord God reminded me of a particular night.

When I was around nine or ten years old I had often been having nightmares. On one such night I had awoken from one of those bad dreams and lay wide awake. All of a sudden I heard an audible voice calling my name, "Catherine, Catherine." The voice was calm and repetitive. I was bewildered and couldn't figure out who it was. I remember asking my sister (who was sleeping in the same room) what she wanted. It was not her calling me, so I remember going to Mum and Dad's room and asking them why they were calling me. It was not them either. At such a young age I couldn't figure out who was calling my name.

I enjoy recalling the memory as it was a calming experience, and I now believe it was an angel of the Lord comforting me right when I needed it. Jesus wanted me to be part of his family, and I am glad that later on I was able to recognise his voice.

Angel in Full Armour

Darren Booth

In November 2012 I was at a home church service/house blessing on a property near Yeppoon, Queensland, and the pastor, Rob Edwards, was preaching about peace and proclaiming it over the household.

As he was talking, I saw an angel of God dressed in full armour standing directly behind him, shadowing all of his movements. When he stepped forward, the angel stepped forward behind him, and so forth.

God showed me that peace has to be enforced with the highest authority, which is Jesus. Just like peace-keeping armies have to take over areas to bring peace, God's peace-keeping angels have to come in to force out the enemy to bring peace. When I told Pastor Rob later, he said he had never seen an angel but always hopes that they are there. It was great confirmation for him.

Chatting with Angels

Pastor Dirk Willner

My life nearly came to an aberrant end when I flat-lined in the cardiac ward of our local hospital. What happened next was nothing short of extraordinary as God allowed me an unforgettable glimpse of heaven before returning me to my physical body here on earth.

For the full story of this encounter, please go to my website: lifebeyondnow@gmail.com

Subsequent to this experience, I have been blessed with two visits from angels. This is what I would like to share with you now.

It was seven days after my near-death-experience and the encounter of heaven. I found myself wondering what it was all for; what I was supposed to do with such an experience. I was sitting up on my bed talking to God. I wasn't lying down and I wasn't asleep. I wanted God to explain it to me. I wanted to understand it. My wife, Penny, and my in-laws were there. It was 4 o'clock in the afternoon, and they were asking if I minded them going off for a cup of coffee.

As they left, five angels appeared around my bed and I could see them as plainly as I could see any other person in my life. They were sparkling like party sparkles.

The one on my right then spoke, saying, "What instructions have you got for us?"

I looked at him and asked, "Instructions?? If you want any instructions, go to God. I don't give you any instructions!"

He then said, "Put your hand in my hand."

I remember him reaching out his hand. I was looking at it. Five fingers. I could see everything, just the way we are–except full of this sparkle. I thought, *Well I'll see where this goes*, and I put my hand into his. The moment I touched it I started to speak in this heavenly language. I was speaking to him in terms of what he needed to hear–and as I was doing this, God was speaking into my life saying, "Don't worry about it. You should know. It's scriptural. I'm just giving instructions to you, and all of this is about spiritual warfare, and the devil has no idea what's going on."

So here I am, putting my hand in his, then the other one wanted his hand in mine and I spoke a totally different language again; and each one in turn–so five different languages. As I then finished, they went; they just turned and disappeared. Then there was this sixth angel on the edge of my bed, and I said to him, "And what can I do for you?"

And he said, "Nothing. I'm just here for you!"

And I thought, *That's cool*! I think he must have been my guardian angel.

The next day around the same time, I was having this kind of conversation with God, and again things started to happen.

I was sitting on the bed talking to God, when this bunch of angels came in. They weren't like the other ones though. They were all grouped together, and as they came in they filled the place with anger and rage.

I was sitting, thinking, *Whoah*! *What have I done wrong*?? And I said to them, "Look, I'm new to all this spiritual stuff. If I've said something wrong, you'll have to forgive me."

And as I was saying this, God spoke into my life again and said, "This is what I want you to do with these angels."

I thought, *Do with these angels*?? Okay, obviously not the same kind of angels as before. I didn't realise that when this bunch of angels had come in that they were fallen angels. God said, "Do this: First thing–mute them, shut them up. Don't even get into a conversation with them. Stop their influence." Secondly, "Bind them, so they can't do anything." And thirdly, "Now forbid them to replace themselves. Forbid them, so that what they are doing isn't being done by anyone else."

At that point I was going to jump in and say, "And now send them to hell?"

And God said, "No, don't send them to hell. Send them to Christ for judgement."

So I did that. I went through those four parts and they left.

But it didn't stop there. The near-death (or near-heaven!) experience led to this encounter with angels, as I was praying, hoping, to get some understanding of my heavenly vision. It was as if God was verifying that my experience wasn't a figment of my imagination.

The revelation of spiritual things kept unfolding–including hearing God's voice. Of all the experiences that I have had and treasure, the glimpse of heaven and experience of angels didn't have as powerful a tug on my life as the conversations with God. This is where I feel the closest presence of God in my everyday life.

But in everything, this experience is really all about a visual experience of what our prayers really long for–knowing that God is here, knowing that there is more to come, knowing that God is looking after us, and knowing that God's presence is for real.

Entertaining Angels Unawares

Robert and Margaret Brown

After 10 years of living a 'full on' lifestyle as a drummer in a rock-and-roll band, working as a junior executive with a national retailer, and being married just over a year, my wife and I were blessed with a life-changing experience with Jesus. When this happened, neither our family nor any of our friends could understand it. It was a radical 'new birth'. Until that time, while we had attended church for most of our lives, its impact had been quite superficial. All of a sudden, however, our priorities had changed. I left the band and my wife and I started attending as many meetings as we could, to learn how to grow in faith and to serve the Lord.

One Monday evening following a prayer meeting, we invited a new Christian friend to come to our home to sing and worship. When we arrived at our home, there were two young men standing near the front door. We didn't know them, so they introduced themselves, one saying he was from Bendigo, the other from Geelong. As we were living in Ballarat at the time, we thought that to be quite strange. Further to this, we learnt that they had only met each other a few minutes before we arrived. During the course of conversation, it seemed the reason they were there was because they had heard we 'loved the Lord' (they wouldn't have known we were planning to have a worship time with our new friend, as he was the only one who knew).

Anyway, all five of us went inside, and we proceeded to sing worship songs. As we did so, it was like heaven had come down and glory had filled our souls. After about an hour, we found ourselves laughing and laughing and laughing with pure joy. It was a night that we have never forgotten. It happened 42 years ago! We have never seen those two men again.

Whenever we catch up with our friend, we never cease to recall this unforgettable, unexpected 'God time' in our lives. As Hebrews 13:2 tells us, *"Do not neglect to show hospitality to strangers, for by doing that some have entertained angels without knowing it."*

In retrospect, this significant event in our lives was a special gift from the Lord to reinforce his love and presence. He knew we needed it at the time as we were such a mystery to our families and friends. We felt very affirmed by it.

Amazingly, the Lord called us as missionaries to Papua New Guinea around two years later. There we had several wonderfully fruitful years sharing the Gospel and planting churches. After all these years, I still receive invitations to return and minister to this now 300,000 people of the Huli tribe.

For that memorable Monday night experience 42 years ago, and countless others since, we say, "Praise the Lord, great things he has done!"

Today I Saw an Angel

Rick Jenkins

My name is Rick Jenkins, and I am from Lockhart, New South Wales. I gave my heart to the Lord Jesus Christ back in 1987. I was 33 years old at the time. I served God faithfully to about 2002. Regrettably, I then slipped back into my worldly ways of excessive drinking again.

In 2008 something happened which really upset and rocked our whole family. My baby daughter, aged 15, became the victim of a horrific crime in which the only penalty for the four 17-year-old offenders was an 18-month good behaviour bond.

Around 2010, before the offenders had been sentenced, I had been really pursuing God again, and looking for answers. After hearing the verdict, I felt God had really let me and my family down. I stood in my back yard and asked God in no uncertain terms how he could let this happen. It was in that moment that I felt the Holy Spirit say to me, "Well at least now we are talking." That really blew me away.

I continued talking to God daily after that, and the more I pushed in, the more peace I got about everything. I was at the Culcairn Church one Sunday, and I was really feeling God's presence, when I looked down on the bare wooden floor and noticed what I thought were two or three specks of what seemed to be gold dust. I said, "Heavenly Father, if this is from you, I want more;

if it's from Satan then I rebuke it." I closed my eyes to get back into the presence of God. When I opened them again, there was gold dust all over the floor around me. That was probably one of the first of many unusual things that happened to me in that church.

One Sunday during praise and worship I saw an old giant angel, and he appeared to me to be like a warrior angel. It seemed like he was just resting. He had a beard and longish hair, both of which were white. He wore a long white cloak. I was totally spun out and thought I had better keep this to myself as I might be losing the plot (you know, too many beers over the years!). It finally got the better of me, however, and I asked my friend, Neil Muller, if he thought it was possible that people (ordinary people like me) could ever see angels. He replied, "Yes, most certainly!" I said, "Well, I believe I saw one today!"

Subsequent to this, I have also had another angel experience. It happened as a group of men from the Culcairn Church gathered in Lockhart near the town hall to pray over the town. This angel I could sense better (if that's the right way to describe it). I felt he was at least 20 feet tall, and he seemed to exude great importance in his role. By that, I suppose I mean I felt very safe in his presence.

Mack's Angel

Rick Jenkins

This story follows the previous one.

My daughter, Holly, had a new little addition to the family—a boy named Mack. He had a rough time when he was born. When I walked into the hospital to see him, he was on two monitors and had a catheter in him.

I prayed to my Heavenly Father that he would be perfect and that they would find nothing wrong with him. To my amazement, the following morning he was well, and he had no monitors or wires hanging out of him.

These days, whenever I go to visit my daughter, young Mack always seems to look in one corner of the house. There is never anything there that could get, let alone keep his attention. I say to Holly I believe there is an angel there looking after him.

It is very hard to describe the angels I have seen. They are most certainly white or maybe more sort of see-through. They're not like you would see on TV or at the movies—and there is the feeling of being in the presence of something or someone amazing—a sense of awe. I can't recall ever seeing wings except for the one near the town hall. The shock of what is happening at the time this occurs is really overwhelming. It's like, "Wow, who's going to believe this??" … then you say to yourself that you're best off not telling anyone.

I believe there is a reason God is starting to reveal these things to believers. I may have seen angels and even gold dust, but I know with absolute certainty that all of this completely pales into insignificance compared to the feeling of knowing that you are in the presence of the Lord. I feel if I was giving testimonies and speaking the word of God that I would likely be seeing more of the supernatural. I don't know what God has in store for me, but I am sure God will use me one day. Maybe he is and I don't even know it. I believe we all have the ability to see into the spirit world, but we just have not been taught or encouraged.

Miraculous Rescue

Myrna Frohling

On the 30th May 1996, my elderly mother passed away. The next day we were preparing to make the trip some 600 kilometres to go to farewell her.

My son, Rod, who was 20 years old, had his mate, Greg, with him and they were fiddling around with an old ute they were rigging up as a 'paddock-basher-cum-fox-shooting' outfit. They had the tractor with the front-end loader attached, with a chain around the front of the ute to lift it up. The front wheels were off, and they had intended to place the front of the ute on the wooden blocks. Both had their heads and upper bodies under the front looking at something that needed fixing. Suddenly the chain snapped. As the vehicle fell, Greg was knocked out of the way, but Rod was pinned underneath; the top part of his body wedged under the front of the ute.

Greg quickly raced up the yard some 100 metres or so to get Noel, Rod's father, to come and help lift the vehicle off him. As they came around the corner of the shed, there was Rod standing up, somewhat bewildered as to what had happened. He did not know how he had gotten out. I took him to the doctor to get him checked out. All he had on his back were two scratches from the underside of the vehicle and some bruising– but no broken bones. How he managed to get himself out from under the vehicle is a mystery. The only explanation that we have is that his guardian angel was there to lift the ute off him. Perhaps it was the angel from his grandmother who was there as well? We will never know, but we are thankful to God that he wasn't badly hurt. He does have some ongoing problems with his back but nothing that a visit to a therapist can't relieve.

We often talk about it, but to this day, over 20 years later, we still marvel at God's power in saving Rod from serious injury, or even death. He has gone on to live a fruitful life, has four children and is a leader in his church and community, besides running a successful and busy farming enterprise.

Oh, and the ute was banished to the scrap heap, never realising the dream the boys had for it!

> *"For I know the plans I have for you," declares the Lord,*
> *"plans to prosper you and not to harm you,*
> *plans to give you hope and a future."*
>
> Jeremiah 29:11 NIV

Money for the Meter

Mandee Anderson

While I was driving from Betros Brothers to the AGBW Office, I remembered that I probably didn't have meter money for me to be able to park in Annand Street. Because I didn't want to put no money in the meter and park regardless (as that would be sinful to do, and today, rejecting sin was a priority on my agenda), and remembering the James reading of the morning *"You do not have, because you do not ask ... "* (James 4:2), I proceeded to ask God if somehow he could supply the money I needed (thinking maybe there would be a meter there with some money still on it, for example).

When I arrived in Annand Street, the first meter I stopped at was expired, so I went to the next available one. This second one did have time on it, but only three minutes (and this would not have been enough time for me to run to the bank and back).

I then started looking through my handbag, thinking there could be a coin in there ... and while I was looking, a very black young man in a brightly coloured safety vest walked down the footpath and said, "Make sure you put a coin in the meter," to which I replied, "Yes, I sure will!"

He then asked whether I was right for a coin and I told him I was searching through my handbag to find something. To this he replied, "Let me get that," and with a coin in his hand, immediately put it in the meter. I looked down for the second of him doing so, and when I looked up again, he had gone. He had simply vanished.

I asked myself, "Could this have been an angel?"

My Guardian Angel

Meagan Edwards

In 2004, at 13 years of age, I had an angel experience at night. I'm not sure what time it was, but I knew it was too late for either of my parents to be awake.

I woke up from my sleep and looked over towards my wardrobe where I saw a pure white figure lingering. It was a strange experience because I felt no danger or fear; rather a feeling of inner peace and calmness that someone with great power was watching over me and nothing was going to hurt me. I remember just looking at the figure.

I fell back asleep and in that same night I woke again to see the same pure white figure sitting at the end of my bed, then the figure/angel came closer to stroke my hair and the side of my face, like a mother calming her child to sleep. It looked like it was young, perhaps in its twenties or thirties, and had short hair that came to its neck. Once again I felt no fear, just an immense sense of peace.

The next day I woke up feeling refreshed and happy–just a little confused as to what had happened the night before. Sometime during the day, I went to go and read the Bible. Instead of reading where I was up to though, I decided to flip to a random page. This is what I read–"*I will say of the Lord, "He is my refuge and my fortress; my God, in whom I trust,"* (Psalm 91.2 NIV); and

"You will not fear the terror of night, nor the arrow that flies by day ... A thousand may fall at your side, ten thousand at your right hand, but it will not come near you." (Psalm 91.5-7 NIV)

To me those Bible verses meant a great deal. They gave me a real sense of safety knowing that God was watching over me and keeping me safe. I wrote those verses in my journal in which I shared my highs and lows, and thoughts about my Christian life. One other thing that stood out to me was the fact that in the very next page of the journal the Bible verse for that day was, *"By day the Lord directs his love, at night his song is with me–a prayer to the God of my life."* (Psalm 42.8 NIV)

I strongly believe that the figure I saw that night was my guardian angel. I still to this day (nearly 14 years on), often wonder whether he or she watches over me and sits on my bed every night. Re-reading those Bible verses, I believe the answer is *Yes*! Yes, my guardian angel is with me at night and during the day. I don't always see him/her but when I am home alone at night I know there is no need to fear even when there may be scary/strange noises outside, because God and my guardian angel are next to me and watching over me. Often when I am driving my car or just outside, and I look up to the sky and see the sun's rays through the clouds, I say "I love you too, Jesus." It is a daily reminder for me that I am being looked after and loved.

Tapping on My Shoulder

Edna Vonow

I was lying in bed in the Port Pirie Hospital (in South Australia) suffering from severe depression, when I clearly heard the voice of what I believed to be an angel.

An old lady in the next ward had just died. At the time of her passing I felt a tapping on my shoulder, but there was nobody there. Accompanying this tapping (which had woken me up) was this voice saying, "You are going to get better from now on." The incredible thing is that in a few days I did get better, and prior to that had been unwell for quite some time.

Our Angel Protectors

Graeme van Brummelen
Pastor, River Community Church, Albury, New South Wales

One night after my wife, Roslyn, and the children had gone to bed, I spent some time praying in our small lounge room. When I had finished, I was intending to go to bed too, but as I turned off the light I felt prompted by the Holy Spirit to go to the window at the back of our home. As I went to the window I heard an audible voice say to me to look down the fence-line to the left.

As I looked, I saw a row of angels sitting on the fence. The whole fence-line was covered with these undefined figures, all with a faint glow about them. I didn't look for distinguishing features and I don't recall how they looked–but it seemed to me that they were perched there. The words came to me that God was protecting us and had stationed the angels along the fence-line for that purpose. I was then prompted to look towards our other neighbours' fence-line, and I saw just a fence. No angels.

Previously we had suffered quite a lot of abuse from those neighbours on the left (due to a puppy we had that cried the first few nights in its new home), so when I saw those angels, it was easy to understand why. Seeing them made me feel protected and cared for by God. It was good to know that he was with us in such a way.

As I stood at the window, I was then prompted to look down into the back yard. Our back yard is quite large, and at the time we had some old pine trees in the far corner. It was terraced in three levels–the house and then two other levels. On the level just below the house we had a table with two chairs. It was there that I saw two angels sitting on the chairs around the table. They were huge; larger than the angels perched on the fence. I then heard the Holy Spirit say to me that those two angels were the angels that were assigned to me; to watch over and protect me. I was amazed. Here I was, standing at the back of our house looking out through the louvred windows in complete darkness, and seeing the angels of the Lord watching over us. They appeared to me to be robed in white linen and were very bright.

The Holy Spirit then directed me to look heavenward. It was now about 11pm. It was not just a look to the sky, but one that went completely beyond what one would normally see in the still of the night. I recall seeing stars on that beautiful clear evening, but as well as that, angels warring with demons in the celestial sphere. There was a great war happening, and for whatever reason, the Lord had enabled me to see that as well.

The angels on the fence were real to me, as were the two angels sitting on the garden chairs. I know that I was not dreaming or day-dreaming. I was fully aware of myself, not having been to sleep or off in a trance. I stood at the window as I was led. I often wonder what would have happened if I hadn't responded to God's prompting that night.

What I saw in the heavenlies was more of a vision because it was only a very short time of seeing it in place. I believe the Lord was showing me that angels are always fighting for us–in the physical here on earth, and also in the heavenly realm keeping the work of the enemy at bay.

On another completely separate occasion, our young daughter who was throwing a tantrum all of a sudden stopped her behaviour and just looked straight at me, changed her tone completely, stood up and declared that she could see two angels standing behind me.

Angels are obviously about, but as for when we see them, and why, I don't know–if it is in God's interest to allow them to be seen, then I believe it is his prerogative. It is up to us to believe his intentions in doing so.

> Daniel wrote of an angel, *"I looked up and saw a man clothed in linen ..."*
>
> Daniel 10:5

My Two Angel Protectors

Robin Jaensch

I was in my mid-twenties when I found myself in Sydney on my own for the first time. I had moved out of home and was living with my cousin.

This one particular day I decided to take public transport and go into the city to do all the sorts of touristy things one likes to do in a new environment. I thoroughly enjoyed exploring places like the beautiful Sydney Harbour and the Taronga Zoo. It was the most wonderful day.

Sadly, however, it came to an end and because I wanted to get as much out of the day as possible, I caught the last bus home after dark. Alighting from the bus in the darkness, I noticed that a man had also gotten off behind me, unnerving me somewhat as I knew I had to walk past two vacant blocks in order to get to my cousin's house. I began to walk briskly as I was very uncomfortable having that man walk behind me. Something made me look around, and when I did, I could see that he was hurrying. That frightened me even more.

With great relief I finally arrived at the flats and was desperate to get inside safely, when in walking through the gates I heard the voice of the man behind me, "Listen lady, I don't know who those two burly blokes dressed in white are beside you, but they've got their fists up, and they're looking pretty cranky. One of them is even holding a sword. I'm not coming anywhere near you. I'm going away now."

As he left I felt a sudden surge of peace move through me. It was warm and special and I knew that God had sent his angels to protect me in that potentially harmful situation. I was very grateful that those angels were there at just the right time, and huge relief that I was not hurt in any way.

I was later to discover something so brilliant in relation to this event that I will never forget it. It is to do with my grandma, and the thanks I owe her will have to be delivered once I get to heaven and am able to see her again.

My grandma had always been a very special lady in my life, and, in fact, in the lives of all her grandchildren. She used to pray for all of us at least once a week. The week, however, and more specifically the exact day of my incident, she felt the inexplicable urge to pray for me and not to stop until she felt in her heart, through the power of the Holy Spirit, that I was okay.

This was revealed in one of the last conversations I had with her before she died. When she happened to mention the date of her ardent praying (I had not previously told her of the incident for fear that it would have worried and upset her too much), it happened to be that exact date.

I know for sure that without the prayers of a loving grandma, and the care of a gracious, loving God, that day could have ended up way more differently than it did.

When I get to heaven and see my grandma, she is going to get the biggest, warmest hug I can muster up. She is one special lady, and I am so glad she knew how to listen for God's voice and to act faithfully on it.

Not Yet His Time

Edna Randall

My father was mowing the lawn with his ride-on mower at a home by the sea. The mower didn't seem to be working very well and was stalling a lot. All of a sudden, on the upward steep slope of the lawn (which dropped away on a bank above a bitumen road beneath it), it lost power altogether.

Suddenly Dad found himself going backwards down the steep slope, and within moments he had fallen to the road below, a distance of about 15 feet. He had landed very heavily on the cement kerb, with the mower on top of him. Amongst other things in that catastrophic accident, he suffered head trauma and eight breaks in five ribs.

We travelled several hours to be by his side in the hospital, but on our arrival were told we could not enter the ICU as the doctor was with him at the time. It seemed like hours had passed before we could see him, and when we did, he was mostly sleeping. I sat there and held his hand, knowing it was important just to be there for him.

Finally he returned home, and during a chat one day he told me that while he was in the hospital he had seen some angels. I laughed at this, thinking he was having a joke with me and that he was simply referring to the nurses who were taking such good care of him–but he said he really *had* seen angels. For my dad to say this was very much out of character, as prior to this he had never believed in such things at all.

Apparently the day we had arrived to see him he had lapsed into a deep coma from which the doctors had been unable to revive him, and he had slipped away. The doctors were working frantically to bring him back at the time we were waiting outside.

It was during this time that Dad said he had found himself in a dark place with a small glowing light far in the distance, and that he seemed to be travelling along a tunnel until he had come into the lit-up area. Upon arrival, he said there were three men standing in long white flowing robes, one asking, "Who is this?"

Another said his name.

The third asked, while consulting a large book, "What's he doing here? He's not meant to be here yet. He'll have to go back!"

At that point Dad said he woke up to see the doctor bending over him and hearing him say, "Well it looks like they didn't want you up there then, did they?"

Rescue in the City

Wendy Millan

The year was 1975. Marcia Hines and Sonny and Cher were on top of the charts. Fashion at the time was bright coloured corduroy pinafores and the classic shirt dress of double-knit polyester. The Vietnam War was coming to an end, and life for me was carefree, spent with friends and socialising.

One night during this time, my friend, Sharon, and I decided to go for dinner at a new hotel that had just opened up. We enjoyed a lovely meal and sat talking for a couple of hours, waiting for Sharon's boyfriend to come and pick us up.

The hotel was closing its doors at 10pm and since Sharon's boyfriend had not yet arrived, we decided to walk the couple of miles home. We were walking along a brightly-lit main highway when all of a sudden we noticed a car following us. It kept stopping and starting, but Sharon and I weren't too concerned as we were busily chatting about anything and everything.

Suddenly it stopped right beside us, and we had just reached an area where there were no houses to run into. It became obvious to us then that they were following us. They did so until we reached a set of closed shops where nobody was around. At that point, one man got out of the front passenger seat and another got out of the back and ran towards us. We were very frightened. I looked up and down the highway for help, but, incredibly, there wasn't a car in sight. The two men who were in their late twenties/early thirties were very drunk.

Sharon started to run across the road in front of the parked car. As she did so, the driver accelerated and hit her, and she fell to the bitumen. I was right behind her and grabbed her as I was running past, dragging her to her feet. We ran for the other side of the road where there was a service station on the corner. I could see a lady walking around a car sales yard which was on the other corner of the side street. I know some of us have had dreams where when we try to call out or scream, nothing comes out, and this was happening to me for real. Eventually I managed to call out, "Hey lady!"

The lady immediately could see the car with the three men inside screeching their wheels, then doing a U-turn to come back and get us. She calmly told us to get into her car, which was a Morris 1100. We just managed to do this and lock the doors, when the car with the men in sped past.

What happened next was something so amazing I will never forget it. The lady turned to us and said, "You girls live in Cowap Street. I'll take you home." We had never met this lady before. At the time I was too upset to acknowledge what she had said, but she dropped Sharon and me right back home. I came to the conclusion that God had sent an angel to protect my friend and me that night.

Later on I got to thinking about what had happened. Whether or not this lady in fact knew us, without us knowing her, I believe that she was sent by God to protect and save us. I believe she could have been an angel, but if she wasn't, she certainly acted as one. How blessed I am to have God as part of my life!

Saved from Drowning

Robert Brown

Some years ago, whilst enjoying a family holiday at Lake Tabourie on the south coast of New South Wales, I decided I would like to try catching the waves with the blow-up surf mat we had recently bought our son, Stephen. I could see that he was thoroughly enjoying himself and I wanted to have some fun too.

Being the 'big' adventurer that I am, I paddled out quite a distance to catch a big wave, only to find myself being drawn rapidly out to sea in a huge rip. I could see the people on the shore becoming smaller and more distant by the minute, and realised that my fierce efforts to paddle back to shore were having no effect at all. By this stage I was really panicking, and cried out loudly to Jesus to save me.

In that instant two men suddenly appeared, one on each side of me. The first calmly said, "Relax, lie flat and still; we will look after you," while the other grabbed the front of the surf mat and strongly swam, pulling me in. The one who had spoken swam alongside and spoke comforting words to me the whole way in. In absolutely no time at all we were in shallow water.

They then asked me if I was okay, but as soon as I called out, "You saved my life … *thank you, thank you!*" they had disappeared.

For days I was totally amazed and overwhelmed by this

experience, and even recalling it today makes me well up with great gratitude to the Lord, and the power that is present in the name of Jesus. I believe those two men who saved me that day were angels sent by God.

The angel of the Lord encamps around those who fear him,
and delivers them.

Psalm 34:7

The Angel Choir

Lois Salzke

I lost my brother in a tragic accident just a few days before his 19th birthday, and three and a half weeks before Christmas. In April our son was born, and three months later my dear father-in-law suddenly passed away. All this in eight months was a lot to cope with. Christmas came and went. The next one was almost here again but I wasn't feeling very well at all.

During the night some days later, I heard the most beautiful singing. Then there was a very bright light ahead–so bright that I couldn't look at it. On either side of this light I could see in its brightness what looked like angels … lots of them. They were glowing and it was they who were singing so beautifully. Then coming towards me were my brother and father-in-law. I began to run towards them calling, "Brian! Dad!" and then suddenly everything disappeared. At that point I woke up.

I believe in this that I was privy to a view of heaven, and while it was just a short glimpse, I rest assured knowing that my family is safe in a wonderful place.

He Kept Me Awake

Colin Letchford

In 1968 I had the job of driving cars from Brisbane to Biloela for a car dealer.

I was flown to Brisbane by the company in the first place, and upon arrival there at 5pm, had to catch a taxi to the other side of the city. The cars for collection were left in the street for me to pick up. I then had to drive home all night.

The first time I did this I got so tired I pulled up at a motel. While I could have just slept in the vehicle on the side of the road, I was afraid to do so because of the number of murders that had recently taken place between Brisbane and Mackay (people had been shot while they had slept in their cars and caravans). Staying in the motel, while safe, did cost me 20 dollars and since I only received 20 dollars for that trip, ended up making no money at all.

Once again, with the next trip, I became too tired to drive. I was wondering what to do when suddenly, out in the middle of nowhere, I came across a man standing on the side of the road. I felt I should pull up, and he hopped into the car. I asked him where he was going, and he replied, "Oh nowhere in particular."

He travelled with me for the next two to three hundred kilometres, and we talked about church the whole way. When we got to Biloela it was three o'clock in the morning, and the only place I could give him to sleep was the cubby house. We had a mattress in there that the kids used to play on, so I gave him that.

In the morning I got up and asked him if he'd like a cup of tea. After boiling the kettle and making my way back out to the cubby house, I discovered that in those three minutes he'd disappeared. Now half a mile around I could see–and he was not anywhere. So where was he? *What* was he?

Since then I have learnt about how you can entertain angels without knowing it–so in my opinion he was an angel. God knew I was tired so he sent this angel to keep me awake during my trip. That's what I believe it was.

The Trumpeting Angel

Darren Booth

In 1999 I went on a missions trip to the Philippines. I was a new Christian, and before I left asked God to help me see into the spiritual realm. God truly opened my eyes. I was made fully aware that there are not only angels that God uses, but that there are also angels that have fallen and become demons.

We encountered one such fallen angel. It followed us around, and we felt a heaviness over us the whole time. I became very sick with a fever, and as a team we prayed for God to make us aware of the name of that fallen angel so that we could pray specifically against it. God answered our prayer with a name, and almost instantly I began to get well.

The next day we were in the house and I could hear this amazingly beautiful music. I asked everyone three or four times if they could hear it, but no one could. I had a strong urge to find where the music was coming from, and so I went outside. There on the peak of the roof was an angel of God playing a trumpet. I told everyone to come out, but no one else could see or hear him. I really believe that in the sending of this angel, God was proclaiming his sovereignty and a fresh new beginning over this place.

The Boy with the Glow

Geoff Severin

When I go through an airport, I have a standard routine in that after I have checked in my luggage and received my boarding pass, and before proceeding through security, I take off all my valuables such as watch, wallet, phone and camera, and place them in my cabin bag. This is to ensure that there are no loose items in the tray.

Well, as usual, at the conclusion of a missionary assignment in West Africa, I went through this procedure. I placed my carry-on items on the belt, and as it went through the x-ray machine, I walked through the personal security hoop. I was met at the end of the belt by a large man who took possession of my items, and informed me that he was a customs officer and that he wanted my money. There was only one other person around, and he was watching the monitor of the scanner.

I told the customs officer that I had no money on me, as before I came in I had left it outside with my friend. He did not accept my answers to his requests, and told me that because I was going somewhere I would have money on me. He then proceeded to give me a 100 percent body search. I had left a small New Testament Bible in my pocket, but he was not interested in that. He then went through my small backpack with my 'survival' kit in it. On finding nothing, he proceeded to go through my zipper-topped business bag, even checking the small zippered pockets in each compartment. Following this, he went onto my cabin bag. The only compartment he did not check was where I had placed my valuables. Finally he gave up on me, and let me go.

On arriving in the departure room, I proceeded to dress myself and then go through my check-list to ensure I had all the small items back on my person–camera, wallet, watch, *passport* and *boarding pass*?? Hang on! I remembered that I had problems at the passport control check-point (she had wanted money before stamping my passport). The items were in my hand when I went through security, and the customs officer, in the confusion, had taken it off me. I'm sure if I had been connected to a heart monitor at this point it would have disintegrated! Without my passport and boarding pass, I wasn't going anywhere. I realised I would have to go back to that intimidating man again.

Just then a small boy came beside me, and handed me those two vital documents. He said he had found them, and thought they belonged to me.

When I had boarded the plane and sat down in my seat I was shaking and crying, but in that, also had such an overwhelming sense of peace and strong sure feeling of the presence of God, that I cannot find words to adequately describe it.

Returning to the boy for a moment ... I was sitting in the middle of a very large room, filled with more than 30 people, when he came from behind. How would he have known that what he had was mine? When I looked at him, the thought that flashed strongly through my mind was, *What are you doing here?* This thought was extremely powerful and it is hard to describe. He was different, and somehow I knew that he did not belong there. He did not fit the scene. There was a type of natural brightness about him. He was only a little over eye-height when I was sitting, probably around 12 years of age, his appearance was different, and he spoke perfect English (which was odd in a French-speaking country). I momentarily glanced at the passport to recognise that it was mine and then looked back to thank him, ask him where he had found it, how he knew it was mine, who he was etc., but he was gone. He was not anywhere in that room. In a way I felt I knew the boy, but was not given the chance to identify him. It was only after I reflected later that I realised what had happened. I believe he was a special angel sent by God! I can remember the incident as if it only happened five minutes ago.

I also reflected on the overall scene in that room as to how God on occasion must open the eyes of some, and close the eyes of others. What did the other people in the room see or not see?

I share this incident with you that you may be encouraged in the absolute truth of the scriptures, and the reality and presence of God in our lives. There can be situations where we have to have the experience, as traumatic as it may be at the time, to receive the blessing. As I reflect back now from the safety of this room, I realise that I was blessed and encouraged in an amazing way through this experience. In sharing it with you, it is my desire that you, too, may also be partakers in this blessing.

... he has said, "I will never leave you nor forsake you." So we can say with confidence, "The Lord is my helper; I will not be afraid. What can anyone do to me?"

Hebrews 13:5-6

Almost Certain Death

Robert Mills

It was sometime in the late 80s (we aren't quite sure of the date) when we had what can only be described as an angelic encounter that saved our lives.

We were travelling north from Melbourne to our new home in Rockhampton. There were five of us–husband and wife, Robert and Yvonne, and our three young sons, all pre-teens at the time. We were driving a large Nissan Urvan pulling a camper trailer behind us.

We had driven so long that we were almost in a daze, when we approached something you don't see much anymore–a one lane bridge with the give way sign against us. We were suddenly shocked to see a large truck already commencing over the bridge, and there was no way either of us could stop. Under ordinary conditions there would have been a terrible crash with awful consequences.

I did the wrong thing and automatically slammed on the brakes. At about 100 kilometres per hour the trailer should have jack-knifed, and the van either hit the oncoming truck or crashed into the dry creek bed over which the bridge was built.

All we could do was to call out the name of Jesus, and a blinding white light flashed across our windscreen which at the time was from the oncoming truck.

I recall that we stopped absolutely dead at the edge of the bridge with no inertia–no throwing of bodies against windscreens etc and slightly to the side of the road so the truck could pass safely, and I have a vague impression of a weird look on the driver's face! I wonder what he might have seen. But he didn't stop.

Our eldest son, who was sitting in the back of the van, called out to us and asked if we had seen the two big men—one holding the camper trailer and one holding the back of our van. I personally had a bright afterglow on my eyes of very large figures holding onto us tightly. The whole episode was over in moments.

Some years later we travelled to that bridge and realised how narrow it was and how deep the riverbed. I have no doubt we saw guardian angels who were sent by God to protect us from harm that day.

The Gowned Figure

Colin Letchford

I had been on drugs for a number of years for a serious health problem, when the resulting breakdowns, crying and having all sorts of awful things entering my mind became too much for me. I was in a terrible state and I knew I had to do something about it. I decided to try to go cold-turkey.

This was not, however, until something incredible happened to me. During my sleep one night I awoke to see this person standing beside me. He was in white clothing and about six foot tall. My wife didn't know anything about it. This figure did not say anything to me but I sat up on the side of the bed and faced it. I couldn't see any features but saw that he was dressed in ancient clothing; a gown.

It was after this experience that I was able to just stop taking all the drugs that were causing me such problems. It gave me the strength I needed for my very difficult situation.

The Guards

Name withheld

There was a time when I was very ill, and in retrospect, was in fact dying. At first I didn't know what was going on. I tried to move but nothing happened. Then the fear crept in as I realised what was happening. I felt myself lift out of my body and look at the ceiling where there was a black hole swelling.

Once on the other side there were two very tall men, about eight foot high. They were dressed in grey hooded clothes, and were serious and stern. They spoke to me, telling me that it wasn't yet my time; that I still had things to do. I pleaded with them to stay, but it was to no avail. We were in front of heaven and those two tall men were guarding the gates.

I was then pushed back into the black hole and into my body with a massive force, and at great speed. Then I remember taking a deep breath, gasping, and sitting up. I went into the room where my two-week-old son was crying, picked him up and cuddled him on the bed.

I left my body again for a second time and was touching the ceiling with the black hole in front of me, then returned once again to my body, this time to stay. Where I had been was very peaceful and loving; a completely different world to what we know here. The only way to describe it is as 1000 birthdays and the happiest day of your life put together.

The Smiling Angel

Kathy Wendt

I was very sick, having been diagnosed with Hodgkin's Lymphoma at age 30. I had a new baby and a five-year-old. After six months of chemotherapy, I was given the all-clear by the doctors.

Eight months later I was re-diagnosed, and was told I would need another six months of stronger treatment, as well as having a stem cell collection. This collection took place in the second month of my next bout of treatment. It involved having twice daily injections for 10 days to stimulate my stem cells to come out of my bone marrow and into my blood stream. I had to have an initial weekend in hospital to have a high dose of chemotherapy administered, then the 10 days of injections, followed by a stay in hospital to check that the amount of stem cells in my blood was right for collection. They were then collected via a dialysis machine over several days through a central line that they had put in my chest. I had become unwell with a migraine due to the injections, and they could not give me any pain relief as they had to continue to monitor my temperature and did not want any incorrect readings.

This is where my angel story begins. I was in a special room by myself with one or two nurses always in attendance. I was not to be left alone as the machine filtering my blood required constant monitoring. I was feeling very low and just started talking with God. At one point I realised I was alone, as the nurses had left the room. This had not happened before. I then looked across the room and realised with my spiritual eyes that there was a huge angel standing across from me. He was as tall as the indented part of the ceiling above the bed (probably around seven foot something). He had curly blonde hair and beautiful blue eyes. He was looking at me and smiling. It was the most infectious smile I'd ever seen and I just had to smile back. Immediately I felt better, and almost transformed (from feeling crappy) by what I was seeing. I then noticed his arms, which were crossed in front of him. He had huge forearms, and I was wondering why they were unusually big. It came to me straight away that these were what he used to wield his sword–of course they would be big!

I also noticed that he was wearing a white tunic, and that he had a big pair of wings which were taller than his shoulders tucked neatly behind him. He did not say anything to me, but just stood there smiling. I felt an amazing sense of peace in that God and this angel knew all that I was going through, and that I was not doing it alone. It gave me an incredible mental boost, and I just rejoiced and thanked God for this special gift at such a low point in my life.

A nurse came back into the room then and noticed me smiling. She said, "What's up with you?"

I just said I felt better. I could not tell her what I had just seen as she probably would have told me I was hallucinating or something, and I did not want any patronising to spoil what had been an amazing experience for me.

I was able to hold onto this immeasurably uplifting encounter through the rest of my treatment, which was shorter that it was supposed to be. That is another story where God spoke to me and told me I had been healed. I still had several months of treatment to go, but as God's word *is* his word, it was true and I didn't need any more treatment after he told me that.

I have many testimonies of his goodness throughout that time, and more. He is such an incredible, wonderful God. Our words do not do him justice.

The Rescue

Di McClelland

It was raining just enough to wet the road. I was coming back over Willans Hill with all my maths teaching stuff when it happened–the car suddenly taking on a direction all of its own and rolling down the hill sideways. I braced myself against the ceiling until it finally came to a stop at a 45-degree-angle in a contour ditch. I couldn't get out; the door being jammed hard up against the dirt. It was balancing there so I sat very still.

"Please Father, put the car back on its four wheels," I said.

It seemed to me then that a great big angel pushed the car down so that it sat safely on all four wheels again. I sat very still, hoping that the car would not burst into flames.

Two tradesmen came sliding towards me. "Are you okay? We saw your headlights in the bush." When did the lights come on? I know I hadn't put them on.

The men used their mobile phones (unusual in those days) to get the police and the ambulance. The police said that there was oil on the road, so they wouldn't charge me with negligent driving. Whew! The car was a write-off, but I was okay.

I know you are always with me Father. Thank you!

Two White Figures

Hilary Park

I was 17 and on my first missions trip. Together with about 20 others, mostly young people, we had travelled to the mountainous area of Papua New Guinea for two weeks.

On the second leg of the trip we were all exhausted and morale was wearing thin. We were at a particularly remote little town, where it was rumoured that there hadn't been white people for 11 years or so. Because of this, we had some fears. It wasn't a personal thing, as the locals were very generous and accommodating, but as soon as it turned dark we would start feeling uncomfortable and scared.

On one such night, my friend pulled me aside to ask if I would accompany her to the toilet. Now the toilet was actually a hole in the ground with a box on top, in a little sectioned-off area a little way from the hut where we were sleeping. This was not uncommon to us, and we had grown quite used to it; however, the night was black and silent and the landscape dry and stark. As we started off, we met with another needing to go as well. There were three of us then, none of us admitting our fear, but all taking our sweet time to put on our shoes; stalling. We set off.

After a bit, as we looked toward our destination, we could see two immaculate white figures standing beneath a huge mango tree (the only tree for miles) right next to the toilet hut. These figures were white from top to toe and very tall. There was no pure white like that anywhere else in the vicinity. We all looked at each other to reassure ourselves that we had all seen it, and of course when we looked again, a moment later, there was nothing–no sign that there was anyone there in the first place. We didn't see them arrive, we didn't see them go, we couldn't see their faces or make out any details–but we all saw the same thing. Our fear left immediately. In its place was an incredible sense of confidence and spiritual awareness.

Journeying with My Angel

Brad Nielsen

One night back in 1993 I went to bed very early compared to most nights, around 6pm, feeling very fatigued, run-down and anxious.

1. The Angel Comes

As I was drifting off to sleep, I felt as though I was awoken to a sound not only that I could hear, but also feel. A vibration went right through me. I realised that I was in a corner of my room, looking slightly downwards across the bottom end of my bed. I was out of my body at that point, looking back at my body still breathing as normal, and asleep.

I could hear a voice coming from behind me, but as I could not see anyone there, remember feeling a bit taken aback by it. The words I heard reassured me that I was safe and in good company, and as they were spoken, a very strong, soothing, magnetic feeling of love and compassion came over me.

A bright orb-shaped sphere then moved from behind me to in front of me, on my right side. As it did so, it changed its shape and appeared before me as a genderless angel. I was somewhat daunted by this, and at this point really took notice that I was floating about one and a half metres off the ground.

The angel continued talking to me but without using its mouth to speak the words out. At this point I knew we were conversing telepathically. I remember the angel telling me that it was there to teach me things. I also remember that at one point I had a strong need to test this spirit to make sure it was a good angel sent by God. I asked, "Do you love the Holy Spirit?" to which the angel just smiled and quietly looked at me. At that moment I had this rush of overwhelming, loving energy go right through my soul. I knew instantly that it was the Holy Spirit's confirmation that it was one of God's divine angels sent by him.

2. Hell

The next thing I remember was being in the upper level of hell and feeling very anxious (like my gut was tied up with fear). Below me was a long shaft that went way down. I couldn't fathom why I would be there, since I loved the Lord so much. At that moment, the angel, whose presence was extremely reassuring for me, said that I had to experience hell first before moving on. The moment I thought of Jesus I was taken away from there. Only God knows why I had this experience–but what I do know for sure is that hell is real.

(Note: I have to say that I don't remember how we got there. I truly, at this point, cannot remember if we travelled to hell or if the experience was brought to me.)

3. Leaving My Room

The angel then took me up into the sky, talking the whole time about things on earth. I remember looking down at the ground and being able to see all the trees so very clearly. Even though it was night-time, my vision could see the whole spectrum. The trees appeared in x-ray form and I remember the angel explaining to me that they were like the earth's living antennae. It's funny, but when I was being told this, I felt a sudden connection to them.

The angel showed me how quickly we could travel just by our thoughts. We would think of a place and within less than a second we would be there. Time was non-existent.

Just on the outside of our atmosphere, I noticed some bad spirits looking down on earth. The angel told me that because of God's love for me, they could not harm me. I remember one of the bad spirits looking over at us, but I knew it was too afraid to approach. The angel said it was the furthest the bad spirits could come out from earth, as they were bound there.

While we were out in our solar system I could feel musical notes coming from all the planets as they spun on their axes. Earth gave off a very beautiful high pitch vibration and I could hear/feel Saturn right through the solar system. Saturn gave off the strongest pulsing low base vibration and it was extremely soothing.

The angel then took me to a mountain on a planet which was unknown to me. On the side of this mountain was a very large house under construction. It was overlooking a beautiful green valley that was alive with trees, plants, grass and sunlight. The angel took me inside where I met the spirits who were building it. We then looked out through the stud beams over the valley when the angel said, "This mansion is being built for you to live in when you return." I could not believe what I had heard. The view from it was absolutely breath-taking!

> *... no eye has seen, nor ear heard, nor the human heart conceived, what God has prepared for those who love him ...*

1 Corinthians 2:9

4. Seeing God's Art-work in Heaven/the Universe

From there the angel took me to see God's artwork out in the universe. He showed me many spectacular images, and I was able to see all the much higher more-alive reactive colour spectrums than what one normally sees. I saw all sorts of images and amazing colours in many gas clouds (nebulae), even including an image of Jesus' face.

5. Reunion with Past Family and Friends

After that the angel took me to what I call the 'grand building' or 'grand temple'. I am not sure of the name of this place but it was brilliant white like a palace. The front was spectacular. There was a beautiful large garden there, filled with ponds of crystal-clear water. The verandah was enormous and had many massive white columns on it.

Once inside I noticed that it was 'alive' with reactive light energy. I cannot put into words how beautiful it was. At one stage I looked up at the ceiling in one of the large rooms and noticed that it was clear like glass. I could see all the stars and universe above. Talk about magic! I was in absolute awe of that place.

The angel then took me into a large room, and as I entered there were a lot of people there waiting for me. I was being reunited with ancestors and friends who had passed over. The feeling I got from everyone there was just so overwhelming with love that it projected from them into my soul, and vice versa. They could feel all of my emotion at the same time as I could feel theirs. My great-grandparents from my mum's side came and introduced themselves to me, as well as my grandfather who had died when my mum was only nine years of age. I noticed that most of the spirits were in the form of light sphere shapes but even though we could not see each other's faces, we knew who everybody was. I remember one male person who wanted to talk to me, and he was at the back of the room. As soon as I thought and looked at him, we came to each other as fast as you can think. While I do not feel ready to say who he was, I can say that he was one of my family members.

I have to say that the whole time I was in that room with my family and friends, the feeling of love and joy was so overwhelming that it is not possible to find the words to describe it. By contrast, being on earth feels so much heavier and clunkier in our bodies, and I know when we are released and able to take that love energy with us, it can then spread out and expand.

6. Life Review and Future Learning

After I had spent some time with my family and friends, I was taken by the angel to a smaller room off to the right side of the grand room. There I was introduced to two very wise male spirits who wore white robes and had snow-white hair and beards. I loved being in their presence.

One of them asked me about an incident that had occurred when I was about five or six years old at primary school. I felt uneasy about this as it involved being in a fight with a class mate, ending up with me throwing a rock at him. When I didn't answer, one of the wise males said, "The lesson to be learned right here is God the Father knows all your thoughts and intentions at all times. You are a part of him, and he is a part of you."

Just after that I was shown my life review. When it started it was like a holographic image that came up in front of me from out of the surroundings, and then I became completely immersed in the experience connecting my soul as one with it. Something that was revealed to me was how on a number of occasions I had hurt people's feelings without even realising it. God put me completely in their shoes so that I could feel just what they went through. I believe it was to teach me empathy and to not make judgements about others.

7. Meeting Jesus and Future Events to Watch For

After my life review we left the grand building, the angel taking me further out into the cosmos than before. We soon came to a large gas cloud which I could almost touch. We rose slowly up the side of this cloud until we came to the top. As we did so, there was Jesus, floating, waiting for us.

When I saw him, I was completely overwhelmed. There was fear of his appearance, and also a feeling of total respect. He looked different to pictures of him that I had seen from time to time during my life. A golden light emanated from him. His hair was a brilliant illuminated snow white. He wore a glowing white robe with a gold sash that went from his left shoulder to his right hip.

The angel brought me in front of Jesus, where I could clearly see his eyes. They were glowing with bright red plasma-like energy. I admit that I felt more afraid of his appearance at this point and wanted to look down, but the angel told me not to be afraid for the burning in his eyes was the burning compassion he has for all people. I then felt that love and compassion go right through me. It was so positively overwhelming it felt like I had been hit by lightning. That's the only way I can really describe it. I also noticed that Jesus' feet were a maroon brown colour. He then wrapped his arms around me, and as he did so, I could feel his love go right through me. It was so powerful he did not need to say anything to show how much he loved me.

Jesus started to tell me of things to come and what to look out for in my lifetime. I received a totally immersed vision from him–similar to the life review experience. I was shown what my future work careers would be–that I would be employed by the Ambulance Service, then go into the highest level of security for a civilian (diplomatic security at federal and state levels) and back into the health service security work again (all of these careers have since happened for me but I didn't give it much thought until eight months ago).

8. My Guardian Angel Showed Itself to Me

After Jesus had finished showing me these things and more, the angel moved out in front of me and opened its wings out for me to see it completely. It was the most awesome sight. It told me that it was my guardian angel, and that it had come to me because my prayers had been answered regarding guidance about my upcoming adult baptism the following weekend at St Thomas's Church at Mulgoa.

9. More Art-work

After that the angel took me to more of God's art-work out in the universe. The scene that stood out to me the most was what looked like the Lord on a throne, surrounded by seven gold lanterns that represented seven spirits. Others, too, were amazing and brilliantly colourful.

10. Returning to My Body

My guardian angel then brought me back to our solar system where I could once again hear the pulsing sound of Saturn. He knew that I was enjoying this sensation, and so he allowed me some time before he said it was time to return to my body and to share what I had witnessed and experienced with others. I felt sad to leave and joked, "I'm happy to stay if you want!" to which the angel laughed and told me it was not the time for me to stay. I was then sent straight back into my body and the next thing I knew I was sitting up, feeling lit up and buzzing like a three-phase flood light.

I didn't tell anyone about any of this until the following week, when I mentioned it to my mother, my wife, and the minister at St Thomas's Church (Mulgoa, New South Wales) before my baptism.

It has taken me nineteen years to date to get this out and I have now started to share my experience with my closest friends. I had thought all along that people would just write me off as losing the plot, but instead of that, their reactions have been extremely positive. As the Lord is my witness, this is a true account of what happened to me back in 1993.

If you would like to learn more about my experience, please go to this website:

www.nderf.org/Experiences/1david_n_possible_nde.html

Angel in the Mirror

Rachel Bichel

Growing up was sometimes challenging and quite troubling, especially through my teenage years where I struggled to fit in with the 'cool' crowd. At one point during these years, I found myself in a place of despair and thinking that I had no way out of the problems that surrounded me. I needed help.

Being brought up in a Christian home and family (which I am so thankful for), I found myself digging for answers and clinging to hope in prayer and trust in God.

It was one afternoon that I was staying with my grandmother I was having a hot shower and I could feel and see the steam cover the entire bathroom. It was in this moment that I began to let it all out to God and pray in desperation.

God heard my prayer and cry for help. As I got out of the shower, I was drawn to an image in the bathroom mirror. The mirror had been completely covered with steam except for this image that appeared to look like what I firmly believe to be an angel. As I stared intently, I felt this complete wash of peace come upon me. I was so excited and full of joy that I burst out of the bathroom door and yelled out to Grandma, *"I don't have to worry anymore!"*

I repeated these words a few times as if it was God speaking the words for me.

Grandma came running and wondering what all the fuss was about. I'm not sure what my Grandma thought that day, but she seemed happy for me anyway. By the time Grandma came to look at the mirror the image was almost gone.

After this experience all my troubles at that time seemed to fade away and become non-existent. I had complete peace, joy and trust in God that day and gave him all my worries. I can say without a doubt that God came through for me and sent me an angel. I felt blessed that I was given this lasting experience that I will never forget.

Sure, I have had troubles since then (who doesn't?), and it's when I do fall into these difficult times that I sometimes think back to that moment to remind myself of how close God's joy, peace and presence are and that he will deliver me out of trouble just like he did that day.

I encourage you to seek the Lord, be still, read his word, sing praises, pray, and trust in him completely and you will see what God can do for you too!

Stairway to Heaven

Bev Schumacher

On the 17th June 1982, Daphne Elsa Vonow's funeral was held in Crystal Brook, South Australia. Daphne was my mum, and we had the wake at the family home. I went out the front of the house with my friends who had come to Mum's funeral. I looked up into the sky and saw a stairway going up into heaven. Along the sides of the stairway were a lot of angels. My mum was walking up to heaven. When she reached the top, she was gone.

My presence will go with you, and I will give you rest.

Exodus 33:14

On Guard

Vanessa Thompson

I was 19 and sharing a very old house with a church friend. She too, was single. The house was one street back from a major highway, on a busy side road, and had a verandah on three sides. My bedroom also had a door onto the verandah. One night a torchlight shining in my face woke me. I kept my eyes closed as I heard my bedroom sash windows rattling as someone tried to force them open–I normally had them open a bit for a breeze. After the windows were rattled, I heard the footsteps head towards my door and it too was pushed and rattled. The footsteps continued around to the back of the house, and now I was worried as my flatmate always had her windows open. I was praying hard for safety as I didn't know what would happen if he got in–he would land right on her bed! I heard the first window rattling and moving up slightly but not enough to gain entry. Likewise for the second window. When the potential intruder realised he couldn't get in, a few choice words were muttered and off he stomped.

Thank you, God! The next afternoon before youth group, we had all the youth come to our house to pray with us. As we were standing on the verandah praying and facing the driveway and garage, I looked at the garage roof. On top was an angel, about nine foot tall, dressed like a centurion and holding his sword across his chest. Someone asked me what I was looking at as my face had changed–I asked if anyone else could see the angel. Only one other person could. I knew we were always going to be safe with God's angels protecting us.

Christ in Sight

Amelia

Last year when I was in Grade 5, I woke up to see a demon at the door. It was staring at me. Then suddenly it went to its pocket and lifted up a gun. All of the angels crowded around my bunk bed. By now, the demon was standing just inside my room. I was so scared. I called out for Jesus. I had so many questions. *Is this real? Will I die tonight?*

I opened my eyes and at the end of the bed I saw this face. It was a man. He had blue eyes and a little bit of a beard. He was smiling. I instantly knew who he was. It was Jesus. I looked around the room. The angels were bowing down and the demon was reaching for the gun that it had dropped. It pointed the gun at me.

One of the angels near my head had a banner. It had the Lion of Judah on it. Jesus was now facing the battle-field. It was then that I realised that I had to go to sleep. I went onto my side and faced the wall. Out the corner of my eye I saw a dragon-like animal fly through the roof and land in my wardrobe. An angel was there putting a harness on it like it was going to ride it. Then I fell asleep.

Portals in my Classroom

Ethan

Earlier this year in my Grade 3 classroom while I was doing some handwriting, I saw a portal and it was black. There was a dragon that came out of it, so I prayed to the Lord that he would send some angels to help me defeat it. I started to help the angels, but the dragon killed all of the angels. So I prayed for some more angels to come down and there were loads of angels that came down. They all fought the dragon and then it turned into Satan.

He said, "That's enough". Then he walked back into his portal. And there was a portal at the door. An angel asked me if I was alright and I said "Yes", so they went back into their portal.

Part 2

Visions

What is a Vision?

Put quite simply, a vision is a dream with spiritual significance. It is a special sort of dream for the details are so vivid that they can be remembered in crystal-clear fashion many years after the event, as though the event just occurred. In the vision you may get a picture (eg of a loved one in heaven, or of Jesus himself!), a message from God, reassurance and hope (confirming God's presence), a plan for the future, a calling to do God's work, or a lesson to learn.

God's Handwriting

Kayleen Proctor

I had just moved to the town of Rockhampton in 2013 when I decided to place my name with Education Queensland on 'Tracer', so I could begin supply work in local primary schools.

A day or so after registering my name the phone rang, and I picked it up to receive a request from Tracer to go to what I thought was a school called 'Park Avenue'. I was excited to be going to work but I had also received a phone call this day a lot later than I normally would have.

While reversing out of my driveway and driving around the corner onto the main road, I realised that in all my busyness of getting ready that morning, I hadn't really had much time to talk to God.

"Morning Lord," I said. "Thank you for work today." And I began asking God to help me in my teaching and to go before me in everything I did so that the students would see Jesus in me and be drawn to him.

As I started to pray this, I suddenly saw a vision in front of me of what looked like a blackboard with a white pen writing the word 'Parkhurst' in calligraphy on it. "Parkhurst? Am I supposed to be going to Parkhurst?" I asked the Lord. I had a strong feeling God was telling me to turn around because I was driving to the wrong school.

Not knowing what to do as this had never happened to me before, my stomach churned and I quickly pulled over to the side of the road. What was I supposed to do? Where had this hand and writing come from? All I knew was that I had seen the word 'Parkhurst'.

I quickly jumped out of the car and ran into Park Avenue State School. As I went to the receptionist, I gave her my name and asked if they had called me. The receptionist looked at me and politely said, "No, we don't have your name on the list for a class today."

Oh no! Was it the other school, that one called 'Parkhurst' I was supposed to go to? I quickly ran back to the car with my heart racing, fearing that now I was going to have to try to make it to Parkhurst State School after driving all the way to the wrong school. Could I make it in time or would I now be too late and be replaced by a more reliable teacher? This was the question that raced through my mind.

As I turned the car around and drove back, I suddenly realised that God always knew I was heading to the wrong destination but being the gentleman that he is, didn't interrupt my movements. It was only when I spent time with him that he started to show me the truth.

There was only one way I was going to find out if this was actually the hand of God writing me a note or if I was starting to see 'weird things' in my mind. I arrived at Parkhurst State School, composed myself and went straight to the office. As I walked through the door, the receptionist looked up and said, "Kayleen?"

"Yes," I replied.

"I was starting to worry about where you were. Please sign here. Your class is waiting for you."

I couldn't believe it. Not only did I make it on time; I now knew for sure that God had sent this message for me personally.

As I walked through the hallway towards the classroom, I wondered why God hadn't told me sooner that I was going to the wrong school. When I thought about it, I remembered the Bible verse, "*You have not, because you ask not.*" (James 4:2). Of course ... I didn't ask him, did I? Our Heavenly Father works through the prayers of his people, and he expects us to ask! Jesus said the Father already knows what we need before we ask (Matt. 6:32), he also knows our desires, but he still requires that we ask him for those things.

The Blue Van

Pastor Rob Edwards

I went through a stage in my life where I started to notice a number of deja vu kinds of moments. After a while I realised that it was because I was having some basic premonitions in my dreams. I would dream short, vignette kinds of skits which would be played out the following day. They were nothing major, and barely noticeable. I was working as a mechanic for a small firm at the time, making orchard equipment. I would travel around repairing and servicing the machinery that they made. Sometimes I had dreams about fixing something, and the next day I would fix it. So it wasn't anything really to write home about, and easily explained. I could, after all, have guessed that I would be doing half of that stuff anyway.

One night I dreamt that I got into the work ute and headed off to another town. As I drove out the front gate of the factory and headed down the road, I came to a 'T' intersection. It was one of those dreams where you can't stop. As I put my foot on the brakes, the ute wouldn't stop, and there was a blue van driving along the road. I didn't hit it, but it was a near miss, and I went over the road into the bushes on the other side of the road. I woke with a start.

Come morning, I got ready for work. I was a little unnerved by the dream because I had been having these premonition type dreams. *This won't happen*, I thought to myself, as I wasn't scheduled to go anywhere. The plan as I knew it was for me to work in the workshop on that day. There were no plans for me to go anywhere.

As I walked into the workshop, however, the boss called me over. "I want you to load up a machine and take it to Waikerie," he said. That town was 80 kilometres away and someone needed a machine immediately. Something had gone wrong, and a replacement machine was needed. So I gathered my tools, loaded the machine and got ready to go.

As I got into the ute, I realised that I was living out my dream. *This is a bit weird*, I thought, and I popped the bonnet, got out of the driver's seat and checked the engine compartment. There was no brake fluid in the reservoir. I filled it up and checked the brakes. They worked, but they wouldn't have before long if I hadn't checked them.

I drove out the gate. As I approached the intersection, I cautiously applied the brakes. They worked fine. I pulled to a halt at the intersection as there was a car coming along the main road.

It was a blue van!

Transformation

Asau Da Costa

One night in 2005 before I was baptised, God showed me a vision. I had been reading my Bible and gone to sleep when suddenly I saw two angels come out from the sun. Both of them were flying down from the sky into my bedroom where I was sleeping. One angel held my right hand and one my left, and then both angels took me up to fly with them. From up high I was able to look down into my bedroom and see my body sleeping.

The three of us kept flying upwards. This time I was able to see my whole house and my body that was still sleeping. As we continued to fly upwards, I was seeing the whole village with many people, a large crowd in fact, dancing very fast. And then we were flying up again, and we reached up into the clouds. We continued and I could see the stars, the moon and many planets. All of these things I was seeing with my eyes closed. They felt so close that I was almost able to touch them with my hand.

I could see myself flying all the way up to the sun, and we then entered a very wonderful place. It looked like heaven. I had never seen a place like it. The sun was like the gate for us to enter in. After that, both angels kept me there while they flew back to the gates through which we had entered. One angel stood on the right side of the gate and one stood on the left.

Suddenly a very big fire came in a circle in front of me. It came closer and closer when a very loud voice like thunder spoke out from that fire to me. All the words I heard were from the Bible, from the Old Testament book of Genesis, until the New Testament book of Revelation. I do not remember all the words I heard but I do recall, "Repent of your sins, the kingdom of God is near!"

The fire disappeared and then a man with a lightning white robe appeared on the right side of me. He came closer and closer to me and said, "Go back to the world and preach the good news that the kingdom of God is near."

After that, both angels flew back to me from the gate and picked me up from that place–one angel once again holding my right hand, and the other, my left. Our exit point was the sun, where we had previously entered. As we were flying back down, I continued to see the moon, the stars and the planets. Once again, they seemed so close I felt I could touch them with my hand. I saw the cloud, the village that I had seen previously, and my still-sleeping body. The angels then put me back into my body and I woke up. I woke up full of joy and the presence of the Holy Spirit. I just praised God with joy and was unable to control my tears. I had never felt such joy before. I thanked and praised God there in my bedroom, and my tears fell the whole night.

The next day, my heart felt like it was on fire. In the morning I started to share Jesus with my family, and then I began to share in every house in the village. I shared Jesus in the market, I shared Jesus on the bus, I shared Jesus in the school. Everywhere I was, I shared Jesus. At that time, I worshipped, prayed and read the Bible the whole time when I was at home. It really was a time of transformation for me.

Every day I shared Jesus with people. I never stopped for 24 hours except when I did not have people around me. Through this I brought many people to know Jesus. Some gave their lives to be baptised and some didn't. People in the village really wondered about me, and they saw a big transformation in my life. This continues until today.

I have had this vision twice. The first is what I have just told you about, and the second happened in 2011 once I had finished my Discipleship Training School and decided to join the staff of YWAM (Youth With a Mission), East Timor.

May the peace of the Lord God bless you!

Armour of God

Helen Vonow

It was Thursday 22nd October, 2009. Sitting in my green recliner lounge chair approximately 11pm at night, I prayed in response to a conversation I'd had with Chaplain Colleen White regarding putting the armour of God on my principal, colleague, and friend, Dominic. I had recently been appointed to the position of deputy principal at our school.

I prayed, "Lord, tonight I'm not going to read my Bible. I'm just going to sit and spend some time listening to you, to see if there is anything you want to say to me. If there isn't, that's fine. I have a question for you Lord: Am I able to put the armour of God on Dominic? Am I able to ask you for that?"

After a couple of minutes, this picture was given to me: two separate streams of bronze/gold light streaming down towards Dominic and me. We were alongside of each other, yet apart. The streams covered us all over with a gold/bronze colour that fitted us like a glove. It was like God was covering every part of our bodies. The revelation was that only God could put the armour on Dominic; it was not something I could do. I could ask God to put it on, and he would put it on us both.

The vision continued ... God told each of us to sit back down in two large separate lounge chairs. They were like two big cradled hands, and we were small in comparison to the chair. I then realised that they were God's hands. We were to sit in God's hands. He would hold us up and protect us.

And still more ... there was a big dome of white light in front of us. God said, "Sit back and watch me sort out the big things." In the middle of the white dome was 'staffing'– the first big job God was going to sort out for 2010. Alongside of this white dome was a small heavy weight, representing a behaviour issue to be sorted out the next morning. God was saying this weight was a small peripheral thing, and that it would begin hard and heavy, but would be hit with a chisel from the top and would crumble into pieces. It was not something to be concerned about. The thing to take note of was the fact that we were to watch God sort out the big things.

The vision felt like it lasted for about two minutes and then it slowly faded away. That night I slept a solid eight hours, which was the best sleep I'd had for quite a few nights.

Freedom for Samantha

June Wicks

Samantha, a beautiful young girl, was only 16 years old when she died. It was the 4th August 2012. In the previous 11 years she'd had 15 operations for tumours on the brain. As part of a prayer chain in my church I had the privilege of praying for her during this time.

After she died, I had the most glorious vision in which I saw her in heaven in a beautiful white gown, skipping around and saying, "I'm free at last. I'm free at last." It was incredibly reassuring and comforting for me to have had this experience.

So we are waiting for God to finish making us his own children, which means our bodies will be made free.

Romans 8:23 NCV

I Saw God

Maaret Sinkko

In my dreams, I can fly. In one dream I was on the verandah, and I couldn't help but think what a great night for flying it would be. The sunrise was throwing golden embers behind dark brown trees. Stars still shone high in the sky. I leapt off the balcony but at the point where I started to lose my earthbound momentum, the mobile phone in my back pocket started to ring. It was very annoying.

This is when things started to go wrong. Instead of flying, I started to fall … very fast! I knew impact was imminent and pondered when it would be, and whether or not it would hurt. I kept falling and falling and the place grew darker–but not black. When there was no impact, I realised I had stopped falling, and remained suspended. I could smell the sweet earth. It was like nothing I had smelt before, yet I knew it. I can still smell it now.

And there was God in front of me–not in the flesh and bones as I would see you–but he was there looking at me. He was very big. We just looked at each other for a while, then I said, "I love you," and woke up.

At Perfect Peace

Kingsley Vonow

Dad died on the 3rd of July 1994. He was the man with whom I had worked daily on the family farm. He was nearly 62 years old. After illnesses of many sorts over the years, the good Lord had finally called him home. My wife and I were there when the code blue alarm went, and then it was all over. Massive heart attack!

After his passing on that Sunday night, the hardest thing happened. Sure, we saw him at the viewing, but then after the funeral it all went blank. I had been with Dad for 32 years and all of a sudden not only was he gone, but so too was total memory of him. No matter what I did, I could not picture him in my mind. Weeks and months went by and still nothing. It was quite depressing not being able to remember my own father.

....

12 months later ...

Throughout the year my wife, Helen, and I had been travelling weekly to a therapist in Adelaide, and it was at one of those sessions that he got me to completely relax and think of the most peaceful setting I could. What came to mind? What could I picture? The water at my feet rushing in and past from the sea as I stood on the beach. The surf breaking on the beach. Often for me this was a place of absolute peace and tranquility.

A few months later again ...

I was lying on my back on the floor in the passage of our farm house after having just gotten off the phone. We had an undecided issue within our local church. I prayed that God would help the situation sort itself out and then I said, "God, by the way, how's Dad going?"

And there he was!! I'll say it again ... *there he was*!

The most amazing picture (or vision) of my dad was in my mind as I lay there. He was sitting on a big boulder in a creek bed with water flowing past. He had his farm clothes and old farm hat on. He had the absolute most peaceful smile of contentment on his face. He was with his Maker and I knew that only the most perfect peace could make such contentment. To find my dad in the most perfect serene place (just like me at the beach) was such a 'wow' for me!

Ever since then (over 23 years), his picture, though now somewhat cloudy, has continued to be with me.

God bless you all as you read these stories, and may you also find perfect peace and God-given contentment in your lives.

> *I have said these things to you, that in me you may have peace. In the world you will have tribulation. But take heart;*
> *I have overcome the world.*
> John 16:33 ESV

Guidance for Our Mission

Anabel de Souza Lima

I work for an organisation known as YWAM (Youth With a Mission) in East Timor. Just after the war there, we received a visit from one of our leaders, Ken Mullingan, who challenged me to pray about and ask the Lord to help me understand what the foundation for YWAM East Timor would be. So we started to pray and one day I had a vision–something that is not common to me at all.

In the vision I saw a hand which gave both us and our neighbours some seeds. We all received the same ones but when we went to plant we prayed, and asked the Lord how to do it. He then showed us what to do, which seeds to plant near others, which seeds we should plant far from the others or in the sun or in the shade, and so we did. When the harvest came, our vegetables were bigger and more colourful and juicy than our neighbours', and they saw it and asked, "Why are yours better than ours?"

We then went on to explain why, and to tell them that the creator of the universe taught us how to do it and if they wanted, we could teach them, and then they would ask for help. We took this to mean that our ministry in East Timor should start with community development in the seven spheres of society, health, education, technology and so on, and that it was important to base our mission on the Word of the Lord.

Direction for My Future

Pastor Rob Edwards

You could say I was dreaming; technically I was. It was while I was asleep and the story progressed as a dream.

We lived on a farm 25 kilometres out from a country town. If one continued on you would get to the state border, beyond which was Sunset Country, then a huge sheep station (usually fairly dry and no good for farm land) but now a national park.

In my dream (at age 17), I was standing alongside the road and could see quite a way back towards town. There was a long stream of people walking past me from the town. I stopped a few of them to ask them where they were going, and they said that they were on their way to a better place, to a great place out there, and that I should come along. As I had been there and seen what was at the end of the road, I told them they there was nothing out there but desert, that the town was back the other way, and that if they wanted to live they should turn around now and go back the other way. Only in the town would they be safe. Reluctantly, some turned around, but many continued past. Some, however, listened to me but didn't turn around. Instead they stayed to help. Together we were able to assist more people to turn around.

Eventually the job was done. All the people had either gone past or turned around, and as the crowd subsided, I, with my small band of helpers–about eight in all, were lifted up onto what seemed to be a pedestrian overpass (a strange addition to the sparsely populated outback). We were lifted up and from this new vantage point could now see in both directions. We could see those people returning to the town, and we could also see the people finally realising that I was right, milling about on the salt flats of Sunset Country. The big border gates slowly closed as it dawned on them that there was no opportunity for reconsideration. It was then that I was able to spend a bit of time chatting with those who had stayed to help.

As I awoke from my dream, I had a sense that I had not really been dreaming but that I had been receiving a message from God. It was a strange feeling–no sense of waking up, but rather, as though I had been sitting talking with someone. There was no sleepiness to overcome, just the end of the dream.

But this was not the end. Sometime later I attended a youth assembly in Adelaide. To my surprise, I recognised a person there whom I had never met–but who had been in my dream. As the years went by I'm sure I met a few others, but by then the memory of the faces was not as clear as the first few years following the dream.

What I know for sure is this–that I received a vision from God that night. In it he told me that I would intercept people during my life and help them change direction. I would enlist help along the way and through encouraging others, would multiply my efforts. I was assured of help as they were real people in my dream. I knew, above all, that this was a call into ministry. I have since become a pastor in the Lutheran Church of Australia.

My Mother in Heaven

Edna Vonow

I feel that I've been extraordinarily blessed and comforted by having had three incredible visions. They were not just dreams. They were far more impacting and special than that.

The first one I had was shortly after my mother died. It was of her walking down the aisle of the church in a black gown and then upon reaching the front of the church, stepping up into the pulpit and all of a sudden appearing shining white.

As this change occurred, I could hear myself asking her in German, "Wie ist es im himmel?" (What is it like in heaven?) to which she replied, "Heilich, heilich, heilich!" (Holy, holy, holy!). I am sure God blessed me with this vision to give me the wonderful assurance that she is indeed in heaven.

*Holy, holy, holy, the Lord God the Almighty
who was and is and is to come.*

Revelation 4:8

My Husband in Heaven

Edna Vonow

The next one was of my darling husband, Dene, after he also had passed away. He had been sick for quite a number of years. Naturally I was heartbroken when he died, but once again God blessed me with the absolute reassurance that he had been made whole and was with him in heaven.

What I saw was an image of him appearing in great glory. He was standing right in front of me and was like a bright light. He was bigger than I remembered him and his whole body was shining. He had come to fruition in heaven. I recall commenting to him on how much he had grown and how wonderful he now looked.

And the one who was seated on the throne said,
"See, I am making all things new."
Revelation 21:5

Encircling Angels

Edna Vonow

In my third vision, I saw angels. During this unforgettable experience, while I was lying in my bed, I saw the most beautiful angels flying around me in a big circle. There would have been at least six of them and I could see their faces and their wings. Unlike the other angel experiences I have had, this one was not associated with a sad time in my life.

Jesus Comes to Visit

Sibylle Walker

After escaping a domestic violence situation with my two young boys and living in a family shelter for several weeks, I was given a shelter house to live in. I had felt safe in the shelter, but once we moved into the house, I became paranoid. I was very frightened and every night before dark, and again before bed, I would double-check that all the windows and doors were closed and locked. During the night any noise I heard would have me turning on all the lights, and checking everything again. I rarely got any sleep. I was starting to get really ill from the lack of sleep, the stress and the fear.

One night when I woke for what seemed like the hundredth time, having heard an unusual sound, I opened my eyes slowly and saw an apparition in front of me. I closed my eyes and opened them again, as I thought that I was seeing things, but no, it was still there. The apparition was floating in the air, about a ruler's length off the floor, near the side of my bed. It was Jesus in a white robe, looking down at me. He said, "Do not be afraid my dear child; I won't let anything harm you."

The burden of fear left me and I felt such great relief. I fell back to sleep and woke the next morning refreshed for the first time in a very long time. Whenever I feel afraid now, I remember that night and the words Jesus spoke to me.

An Immediate Answer

Ruth Eames

About two months after the death of my husband of 60 years, I experienced for the first time in my life, real depression. I woke up at 1am feeling very ill, alone, and missing my husband desperately. "Oh God," I called out, "I cannot stand this. Help me!"

Instantly I saw a real, somewhat misty image of Jesus in human form standing right by my bedside. His presence was so real I wanted to reach out and touch him, but felt I must not just yet. Radiating from his presence was an overwhelming atmosphere of love and compassion together with a clear message, "You are not alone. I am always here!"

I must have fallen asleep immediately for I woke to see the sunshine in my window. My joy was complete. All the sickness and loneliness had gone. "Thank you, Lord. Thank you."

In the four years since I had this amazing (heavenly) experience I have never felt better. My physical health is declining but the image of Jesus is still so real. It has never faded. My faith and love for him has grown so much because I now fully understand his amazing love for us all.

Living the Dream

Evilasio Oliveira (Youth With A Mission, East Timor)

I will share with you a dream I had which one day later became reality for me.

When I was about 22 years old, despite the fact that I was going to church twice a week and was a worship leader, my life was very far from God.

One Saturday night I dreamt that I was walking with my sister when she saw a room that was on the second floor without any stairs leading up to it. To get there she needed to levitate, which she did. I decided to go there too, to see what she was doing. When I entered, I saw lots of beds and lots of people on the beds engaged in all sorts of debauchery. My sister was praying on the left side of the room. I was not comfortable there and decided to leave.

In another part of the dream, I saw myself walking along a dark path when two policemen came and put me down on the ground. They had some marijuana in their hands, and they put some in my pocket and started to accuse me. Immediately I started to scream for my sister, and for Jesus, and I woke up.

The next day, Sunday, my pastor had gone to another church with some kids for a kids' conference, and he asked my brother to pick him and the kids up at the bus terminal that night, but as my brother had worked very hard during the day, asked if I would do it instead. After taking all the kids to their house, I was going back home with my pastor when one of my friends stopped us on the road and asked for help because his mother was not feeling well. She was, in fact, having an evil manifestation.

It was at this point that I started to live the dream. I entered the house upon the request of the daughter, to help hold her mother (after having stayed outside for a little while as my pastor, who had entered first, had told me to first ask for forgiveness of my sins). When I got to the room, my pastor was on the same side as my sister in the dream, and he started to pray for her. His son asked the evil spirit who he was, to which he replied, "I am Satan." He then asked what he wanted and this time responded with, "I want her." There was a time when the devil said, "I was just one, but now we are seven." This was the part of the dream where I saw lots of people in the room on the beds.

I was so stressed by this situation that I badly wanted to leave the place. However, I also thought I should help my pastor in prayer. I stood up and I started to pray against the enemy. At this time, I started to feel weak, I had vomiting and diarrhoea, and I fainted. My nervous system was shaken.

The next day some children were saying that I had an evil spirit as well. This was the part of the dream where the policemen came and started to accuse me because of the marijuana.

This was a very good lesson for me. From that day I promised to God to just walk in his path and live the life he has for me.

Meeting Jesus

Rev Anneli Sinkko

I have been a Christian most of my life, but it was only as I was worshipping at a Finnish church in Brisbane that I realised with certainty that what has been told of Jesus is really true. The pastor was preaching and all of a sudden I had this amazing revelation from God that Jesus really is alive.

Subsequent to this, I have seen my Lord on a number of occasions. One of those times was when I was visiting with my husband at Cloudland Market. There I saw a man selling shoes, and as he was kneeling in front of a client, all of a sudden this vision flashed across my mind in which it was not this man, but my Lord, washing his disciples' feet. I shared this vision at the Bible College I was attending, and we began a ministry to that market and told people there of our Lord.

Another remarkable thing happened when a couple I had been praying for became Christian. At the time the Lord gave me a vision in which he spoke to me. What was amazing was that he spoke to me in Finnish, my mother tongue, and he said, "*I have called you by name–you are mine. Mountains may depart and hills brought low but my covenant of mercy will never depart from you.*" Little did I know that those words were from Isaiah chapter 43–something I was to find out much later on. At the time I hadn't even read the book of Isaiah.

After that I was filled with the Holy Spirit and spoke in tongues. This is something I will never forget. The whole room was filled with light and I could see him clearly as a person full of light and love. I felt absolutely blessed.

What a marvellous journey I have had with the Lord Jesus!

My Daughter in Heaven

Lesley Bain

The 13th of December 2000 was our second daughter Kara's 23rd birthday. She decided to treat herself by going into the mountains for some rock climbing, which she loved. Little did we know how much of a memorable day it would become for all of us.

Later in the day two policemen came knocking on the door of our house, inviting themselves in. They were the bearers of tragic news ... that while climbing, Kara had fallen from a slippery rock and died.

When this happened, big changes began to take place. Not only wouldn't I see my daughter again on this earth, but also, God began a most amazing and beautiful thing in me. This process started as soon as I sensed what those policemen had come for and I had asked God to help me (as it was going to be too difficult to handle on my own).

Word got around miraculously and the 'prayers of the saints' went up like a flood overnight. An almost tangible presence of God came around me (as well as my husband and our four remaining children). God ministered to each of us in different ways. I myself went on an incredible journey of healing as he spoke to me so personally over those first few days, as I slept, as I read Kara's journals, and as I thought of her over her last year.

In amongst it all, I had four visions:

The first was of her angels. Kara had taught me to believe in her angels. As a young girl, she had described her two angels, telling me their heavenly names as well as the nicknames she had given them. At her death, I naturally became very cross with them for not doing their job, when suddenly the words, "What if that day their job was ...?" came to me, and I found myself 'seeing' the angel with 'the Roman nose and the hair almost to his shoulders.' He was flying in a horizontal position with one arm out in front and so fast that his hair was blown back off his face. His face was focused and intense with determination; a sense of responsibility. I knew that picture was of him taking Kara to heaven and I knew Kara and her other angel were with him as well. They were flying in a v-like formation. I know Kara is safe in heaven.

The next vision I had, somewhere in those first few days, was of Kara dancing before God's throne in heaven. I had enjoyed the sense of heaven many times before in church during worship, but this was the first time I realised that there is no weight of gravity in heaven as I saw her doing the most amazing high back-flips as she worshipped. Then from the right-hand side of the throne I saw these lovely white smiling teeth, and realised they belonged to Jesus who was about to step out and join her in her joy.

Neither of those two visions were very long. The third was even shorter. It only seemed to be for a split-second but it is certainly indelibly printed in my memory. Kara was shimmying up the side of a pile of boulders. Strangely, the boulders were perfectly round and placed almost like a pyramid–except that one face was vertical. From this vertical face she did a back flip into the River of Life, crystal clear, blue and exhilarating. This actually shocked me because she had died from falling from a height, but the River of Life brought such healing.

About two weeks later I had my fourth vision. I was out having a coffee with one of Kara's friends at a place where Kara and I used to enjoy going to, when I kept being distracted by this vision. It was of Kara in a sleeveless red top hanging out from a cloud. She was lying on her side with her head propped up on her hand and leaning on an elbow. Occasionally she would roll over onto her back and then prop herself up on her elbow on her side again. My mind wrestled with this saying that only cartoons depict heaven as clouds like that! But the vision persisted off and on for the next 24 hours. Kara never actually looked at me, just in my general direction. I knew in this vision that God was making it very clear to me that Kara was quite content to be in heaven, and that he was very happy to have her there. This is what I know very strongly in my heart.

He will wipe every tear from their eyes.
Death will be no more;
mourning and crying and pain will be no more,
for the first things have passed away.

Revelation 21:4

God Spoke to Me

Abelita Espirito Santo

There are two experiences I want to share with joy.

The first happened when I was attending the Discipleship Training School for 'Youth With a Mission' in Dili. During the night when I was asleep, I saw someone like an angel dressed in white standing beside me. He said to me, "My child, obey me. I have forgotten all your sins. Follow the next things–believe in me, obey me and hear me." I was so amazed at this that I woke up and started to cry.

Two Big Arms

Abelita Espirito Santo

The second happened after I had finished my Discipleship Training School and had returned home to my district to visit my family. My uncles were very angry with me for following Jesus. I was sad about this, so I went to my room to pray. I asked God to pour down peace into my uncles' hearts. Suddenly I opened my eyes and saw a white cloud that was coming to surround me. There were also two arms opening up towards me. These words then came into my mind–"This is not a time to cry or be sad because I have forgiven all your sins. You no longer live in darkness. Love and forgive your uncles because they don't know what they speak."

The Comforter

Margaret Ward

I have been fortunate enough to have had three personal visitations from God over the years.

The first was as a student when I was 19 years old. I was in the nurses' home at 11pm before going to bed, when word came from the nurses in the corridor that there was a prowler in there somewhere. The doors were able to be locked, but the walls left about three feet of space between the wall and the ceiling and about two feet between partition and floor. I was very scared, but also knew that I had to get some sleep so I could be on the ward at 5am to start sponge baths. I hopped into bed and had my prayer time.

Just as I did so, I saw the person of Jesus sitting on the side of my bed, and he held my hand until I went to sleep. His presence brought me incredible peace. He was white in appearance and like a spirit. While I didn't see him for very long, I knew he was there.

The Bright Light

Margaret Ward

The second happened when I was 40. I had been in Papua New Guinea for 12 years as a Christian nurse but had since relocated to Albury with my husband and children. At that time, I was attending a Pentecostal church. Right in the middle of the service, in the middle of the congregation, a bright light shone down. It wasn't one of the normal lights in the church. I believe that it was the glory of God; the presence of the Holy Spirit in that place.

Seeing Jesus at Communion

Margaret Ward

The third visit from God was at St Peter's Lutheran Church at Gerogery in New South Wales. I had just started to attend there with my Dutch friends, Jack and Gloria Holwerda. We had Holy Communion and Pastor John Borchert was ministering. When he turned around with the bread and wine, I saw not him, but the person of Jesus. This was such a blessing to me, as I was looking for a home church after the sad loss of my church in August 1999. Once again, I recognised his presence. It is difficult for me to explain just what he looked like, other than the fact that he appeared in white.

While I haven't been in the best of health over the years, I believe that God has been keeping me alive and providing me with these experiences so that I can assure other people that he is real.

The Door

Win Perry

This story is about my father, a man of very strong faith and a role model I try to follow.

Over the years he'd had a series of health issues, and one day, upon having had a stroke, we were called in, the doctors thinking he would not survive the night. As we were standing around his bed, he became really agitated and kept saying, "I can't find the door." My mother told him it was okay, and he became calm and drifted off to sleep. It was a few days later, after he had recovered and was on the mend, that he told me this story ...

"I saw a stairway going up to heaven which was so beautiful with pearls and bright colours. I was trying to go up but could feel myself being pulled back. I managed to get away and get to the top of the stairs where I could see many people on the other side of a high wall. I was trying to find a way in, but couldn't find any door (which explained his talk while he was recovering from his stroke). The people I saw were dressed in pure white, and their faces were radiant, and I really wanted to go and join them."

A couple of years earlier we had lost our son at age 13 in a shooting accident, and my father could see him on the other side of the wall, looking radiant and happy. There was so much comfort in that for us, knowing that our son was in heaven!

My father always said he wasn't afraid of dying as he knew where he was going, and it was going to be good. On the day of his death, a pastor had come to give him Holy Communion. As this was happening, his face became incredibly radiant. I believe he had seen his Lord and was happy to go and join him.

> *... they will walk with me, dressed in white,*
> *because they are worthy.*
>
> Revelation 3:4

The Pine Box

Lynne Newbold

This is the relaying of a vision my sister had after our father passed away.

Background –

For most of his life, our father belonged to an organisation which didn't have a recognised doctrine for salvation. As a result of this, when my sister came to know Christ, she alienated herself from Dad because she spoke so strongly against what he believed in. His beliefs totally contradicted the fact that we are all sinners and in need of a Saviour to reconcile us to the Father.

From that point on, it was my idea to ask him questions in a non-judgemental way so as to inspire him to make investigations regarding Christianity for himself. He read his Bible often, but it was nearly all from the Old Testament without getting the New Testament fulfilment in the death and resurrection of Christ, and why it had to happen.

Over time I believe the Holy Spirit began to convict him of his need, for while waiting in the hospital for his second triple bypass, he was unusually optimistic of the outcome. He realised he had a lot to look forward to, not the least of which was the arrival of a new great-grandchild, the first that would carry the family name into the next generation. Normally quite a pessimist, I found this change in attitude quite surprising and refreshing.

Still concerned about where he sat in relation to Jesus, while there on my own with him at one point, I quickly jumped at the opportunity to put an important question to him–"Dad, in the worst case scenario, are you ready? You know it has to be with Jesus, don't you, because he himself said that no-one comes to the Father but through him?" His affirmative reply reduced us both to tears.

A week after the operation he had a small stroke and his leg retained fluid. There was talk of yet another operation, but he felt at almost 83 years of age that he wouldn't be able to take it. Later that night he died. It was a blessing for me to see him looking so beautiful and at peace. He had always said that he didn't ever want an elaborate funeral. "Just stick me in a pine box and bury me out in the scrub on the farm," he said.

....

The vision –

It was shortly after his death that my sister had her vision. It was of a big pine box upon which was stamped the word 'RECONCILED'.

Our family all now believe that our ongoing prayers were answered, and we have the full assurance that we will indeed be reunited with our dad in our next lives.

The Reality of God

Ian Pertzel

Below is a description of the first vision I ever had, which gave me my saving faith in God. I have always considered myself as having had a good Christian upbringing, grounded in honourable principles taught and inspired by my parents and family–but something happened to me at the Hillsong Conference in Sydney, in 2006, which led me to question how much I really knew about the Christian faith, and its deeper meaning.

One night, during the praise and worship session, my eyes filled with burning tears, painful enough that I had to close them to minimise the discomfort. As this happened, I found myself looking, somehow, at a vision of Jesus on the cross. It was very real to me, and seemed as if I was standing there looking at a live scene, not some picture from the past. I had a very real sensation of having been taken somewhere to see what I was seeing. The world around me had faded away, and I stood now in this place instead. A short distance ahead of me I could clearly see Jesus on the cross, on a small mound or hill. There was no one else around, and a light mist was blowing across the scene behind. Jesus was not moving and his head was tilted to one side. He was not messy or gory; there was no blood. He seemed totally at peace, and the scene was very peaceful in general. His spirit seemed to have left him.

While I was watching, I found myself believing in the reality of the Bible. I remember thinking that if I am looking at the crucifixion, at Jesus himself on the cross, then it must all be real. At that moment of acceptance of the truth, I felt a sensation that can best be described as a warmth, like warm honey, being poured into me through the top of my head, slowly filling my being. Gradually it filled me, from the tips of my toes to the top of my head, out to the tips of my fingers. I felt as if the Holy Spirit himself was filling me with pure love, gladness and peace. I felt renewed, healed, and as if all of my earthly cares had been lifted away. That is the best description I can give, as I don't really have the words to describe what happened to me at that time.

It was a deeply moving spiritual experience, and I believe God called me at that time to do his work. I knew then that I would go to Bible College to learn more about the Christian faith, and that from that time I would walk with the Holy Spirit. I bought myself a Bible and have been reading it since. I have started attending my local church regularly, going to a Bible study group, and generally trying to help out where I can. Sometimes I play in the church band. I have been blessed and honoured to be able to preach God's Word, and to share the wonder of God's great love with others. My life since my revelation has been a real joy, filled with peace and purpose, and my church has become my family. I wish only to serve and worship God, to expand my knowledge and understanding of Christianity, and to walk with the Lord.

You are too Early!

Lois Salzke

This is the story my grandfather told his good friend from his hospital bed, just days before his death.

In a vision he could see that he'd gone up the golden staircase and knocked on the golden door, upon which a voice had spoken from within, using his name—"You are too early! Come back on Wednesday at 8am, and I will open the door and let you in."

It came as no surprise to us then, that the following Wednesday at 8am my grandfather passed from this life into his heavenly home.

> *After this I looked, and there in heaven a door stood open! And the first voice, which I had heard speaking to me like a trumpet, said, "Come up here, and I will show you what must take place after this."*
> Revelation 4:1

Part 3

Hearing God's Voice, and More

Serve My People Well

Lee-Anne Kupke

During the night of the 21st February 2011, I woke around 3am to the sound of someone calling my name. It was approximately the same volume as the voice of my 12-year-old son Zakea, who sometimes called out. I knew, however, that this time it was not him. I became alert but not really awake.

When I heard my name being called, I knew in my heart it was God and so replied, "Yes Lord? I am listening."

In response, I clearly then heard, "Lee-Anne, serve my people well."

This happened at a time in my life when I was starting my own business in assessing elderly people in their homes. I have taken this experience to mean that I am to ensure that I am doing God's will in the lives of all the people I see, whether in the community or for work. I think that there are parallels between what happened to Samuel in the Bible, and what happened to me, except I didn't have to remember as much in the morning!

I am the good shepherd; I know my sheep and my sheep know me ...

John 10:14 NIV

A Disaster Averted

Janette Heintze

It was late one afternoon, and my husband, Justin, and I were on the grassed foreshore area of our town having fish and chips with our three children Brodie four, Bethany two, and Lukas six months.

After enjoying our family meal, we let Brodie ride his trike on the ramped stage area. This was a safe area for the kids to play in as it had a pool fence type safety railing right around the perimeter. Several metres beneath that stage was the beach proper, with many large rocks between the sand and the higher grassed area to prevent erosion.

Bethany was happy to toddle after Brodie as he rode his trike. The stage ramp had a low wall both sides, and this prevented me seeing Bethany for brief moments before she would come back into view on the other side. The kids played like this for quite a while and Justin and I enjoyed the moment by ourselves and the baby, while keeping an eye on the other two from a distance of about 20 metres.

A time came, however, when I realised that Bethany had not come back into view on the stage. Accompanying this was the hearing of a not quite audible 'voice' to go immediately and get her. At this I quickly jumped up and ran to the stage area I couldn't see, and there was Bethany standing right in the middle of where one of the vertical posts of the fence should have been. She was looking down and sort of wobbling in her toddler way as she did. Had I not turned up at that moment, Bethany could easily have lost her footing or hand grip, and slipped through the gap, falling five metres onto the boulders below.

Justin's and my faith has grown immensely since that experience ten years ago. When I share this encounter with others I do find it difficult to describe the prompting and urgency that was put upon my heart to move immediately to Bethany. It was not an audible voice from heaven; it was more what I imagine to be a push from the Holy Spirit to immediate action.

Since then, we have added another gift to our family–Liliahna, who is now nine, and one of our favourite family outings is still fish and chips at the beach.

A Life-Saving Nudge

Name withheld

At one time when my dad was working under the house, my mum, Val, had a premonition. She suddenly kicked off her shoes, ran down the stairs, and pressed a button in the meter box. My dad said that this action saved his life as he would have otherwise been electrocuted. My mum had known nothing about electricity meter boxes to that point.

A Word of Comfort

Name withheld

I was alone in my house in Norman Gardens at a time when I was feeling stressed and anxious. A woman suddenly appeared in the hallway and said to me, "Don't worry. Everything will be alright." I was comforted by this and when I asked the visiting Blue Care nursing assistant who the woman was, she did not know her.

A Precious Touch

Robyn Wuttke

Kay's dad had lost his wife later in life. He missed her very much and was very lonely without her. He was a man who loved being outside in his garden watching plants grow, and the beauty of nature all around him.

On the first celebration of his wife's birthday after she died, he felt terribly sad and weighed down with grief. It had been a very hot day so he went out to water the garden in the cool of the evening. While he was out there, a white dove came and landed on the roof of the house. He had not seen a bird like this ever before in his garden.

He talked to the bird with little cooing noises, upon which it then flew down to the tree. He kept on talking to it and it flew down to his shoulder and lightly pecked his cheek for a time. From there it flew down to the ground. Kay's dad told the little bird to be careful as there were cats around. The little dove looked up at him and appeared to check that he was okay, and then flew back to the roof of the house and off into the sky.

What a precious touch of God's love and comfort! His heart felt lighter. He knew that the Comforter had come.

Peace I leave with you; my peace I give to you. I do not give to you as the world gives. Do not let your hearts be troubled, and do not let them be afraid.

John 14:27

A Strange Sensation

Name withheld

It was 2am. The night was very still. I lay in bed, wide-awake, thinking about the life of Jesus and the wonderful truths he bequeathed to us. I then thought about his death, how he had the power to avoid it but how he chose to go through with the agony so he could fulfil his purpose. If he had escaped like a coward, would anyone have remembered anything he did or taught?

As I was lying there, I felt a strange sensation moving steadily through my body from my feet to my head. It was like a movement, but nothing moved. Then a voice in my head said, "You're okay."

It was a special personal experience.

My Father's Transformation

Lois Dunchue

My father was born in 1900, and really had a very sad life, which I think moulded him into the person he eventually became.

He married my mother, a gentle, deeply Christian woman, and they had two children–me first, and then my brother three years later. My mother, even though quiet by nature, had a streak of stubbornness in her and maintained that we had to be baptised, go to Sunday School and receive a Catholic education–and this happened.

My father was deeply opposed to this and fought it every inch of the way, both verbally and physically. I can still hear him saying, "Don't be influenced by what you hear at those places. It is all a pack of lies; just fairy stories." Occasionally Dad would even say, "I have given my soul to the devil."

When Dad was 92 his kidneys collapsed, and for him to continue to live he would have had to be connected to a kidney machine. He decided instead to die, and my brother and I were summoned to the hospital. My brother was living in the same town as Dad in South Australia, but I was living in New South Wales. I therefore flew over to spend his last days with him. The hospital was very accommodating and Dad was able to spend his last days in a lovely restful room overlooking the water, the staff providing every comfort for him and us. I spent most of my time with Dad.

When I arrived, Dad was connected to life support, but it was then disconnected, and he slipped into a coma. I had never experienced anything like this before, especially seeing his eyes cover over with a white substance. Because I knew that hearing was the last sense to go, I constantly told him that I loved him, and so did Jesus, and continued every day to give him the life-changing Christian message. He had always been a very strong, healthy man, and as such his heart just would not give up. He remained in this coma for nearly a week.

Although Dad hadn't spoken for five days, one night I was awakened by him screaming and yelling out, "Get away from me! Get away from me!" Immediately I jumped up and put the light on, and there was Dad sitting up in bed continuing to scream. He was extremely distressed, but the awful thing that accompanied this was the terrible pulsating evil atmosphere I could feel in the room. It was so real that the hairs on my skin were actually sitting up. Instinctively I knew that it was the devil coming to claim Dad's soul.

Absolutely determined to not let this happen, I took off the cross I was wearing and held it over Dad, yelling at the top of my voice, "Get away from him! You can't have him! He belongs to the Lord Jesus Christ! In the name of Jesus Christ, go away!" Immediately after that, Dad settled down and slipped back into bed, still in a coma. The nurses rushed in to see what the disturbance was all about.

Dad lived on for two more days and I continued to give him the Christian message and beautiful reassuring passages from the Bible like, *"In my Father's house are many rooms. If it were not so, would I have told you that I go to prepare a place for you? And if I go and prepare a place for you, I will come again and will take you to myself, that where I am you may be also."* (John 14:2-3 ESV)

When it was actually time for him to go, another most unusual thing happened. His eyes cleared from the milky substance that had been covering them, and he just looked back and forth from my brother to myself. As his spirit departed, I sent his soul on to our Lord Jesus Christ with the message, *"Come to me, all who labour and are heavy laden, and I will give you rest."* (Matthew 11:28 ESV)

It was a most peaceful time, and I instinctively knew that my dad was in the presence of the Lord.

One Last Goodbye

Don McCall

My story ... is it God, the spirit world of popular mythology, or something else?

Having found my faith in Jesus Christ somewhat after my teenage years, my mind from time to time casts itself back through the years to happenings of the past. Having turned one particular instance over in my mind on many occasions in the years since, with various internal theories on, not its reality, but its purpose and cause, I have decided to write about it. I have not done this until now, and it is only that niggling feeling that the story does, in fact, have a purpose, that I am putting this down for others to read and make up their own mind on the meaning of such events.

My story begins in this instance with my having enlisted in the Australian Army at the age of 17. At that time, basic training was carried out at Kapooka at 1 RTB, the training battalion. This was a long way from home for me, having been raised in South Western Queensland on the border with New South Wales, four miles from the town of Yelarbon. My family came from a small farm, something like 110 acres or there-abouts–certainly nothing grandiose in those days, and still not today.

My father had passed away, essentially leaving my mother to cope with four children, one a little older, and the other three around toddler to school age. In fact, I myself was in grade one at school when Dad's unfortunate passing happened upon us. It wasn't really that Dad had not had a very full life, as he was already into his seventies, however, sun cancers and the resultant ill-health resulted in him passing away.

My grandmother lived in Yelarbon, and we children for the most part, at least in our high school years, lived with her in her Burrell Street house, boarded the school bus there each morning to go off to the junior high in Inglewood, and returned each evening. She was a wonderful lady, who had helped us so much over the years that it's hard to quantify. She had a tremendous caring in her for all of us children, but I myself always felt a wonderful affinity with her. Health-wise, she had suffered from diabetes, with the regular tests, tablets, periods of her sugars being out of whack, and as she got into her mid-eighties, a few stays in hospital. In those days there wasn't really much opportunity to stay in an aged-care setting in that region. If you could not look after yourself at home, or your family could not take care of you, you simply ended up at the local hospital.

I had said my goodbyes to my family, including her, for the duration of my basic training, never thinking I would not be seeing her again. Some weeks into basic training, which was of course a very busy time for all of those who were there to progress forward in army life, an incident occurred which even today, some 30 odd years on, still causes the hair on the nape of my neck to prick up!

One evening, quite early really, I had become somewhat unwell.

I took to bed and was wracked with the most awful fever, and then my temperature, or at least my feelings, turned to the most horrible cold. Feeling consumed by the cold, along with the chattering teeth that went with it, I piled all of my army issued blankets onto myself, to little avail. My room-mates, of course, were aware of my predicament, and aided me with the use of their blankets as well.

Some time later, which seemed of course like forever, but was likely to have in reality only been a couple of hours, the cold abated and the shivering stopped. It seemed to be a moment of calm and peace, just before dropping off to sleep. During those few moments before sleep, I had an intense sense my gran was there in that room with me … in fact, that she had stopped for one last time to check in on me on her way to somewhere else. Heaven?? A clear realisation dawned on me in those moments that she had indeed passed on. I then dropped off into a dreamless sleep.

The following morning, I awoke and dressed for the day, and readied for our morning parades and breakfast. Not long after dressing, the communal telephone which was located in each barrack building rang, and I was called to it.

My mother was on the line, her first words being, "Donald, I have some bad news for you … "

My immediate thoughts went to the previous evening and I said, "Mum, I know. Gran passed away last night."

She went on to relay the pertinent details of the circumstance, including the time of death. It was no surprise to me then, or now, that her time of death was consistent with the timing of my cold having abated the previous evening, and the sure and certain knowledge of her passing.

Our Lord gives us opportunities in our life, as we live towards his plan for us. I firmly believe I was given this opportunity to say goodbye one last time. It was a gift not just for my young soul, but also for a gran who had given so much in love throughout her lifetime in just so many ways.

Pinned to the Ground

Pastor Rodney Witmitz

My experience was not with visions or angels, but rather with being confronted directly by God. It relates to my calling to be a pastor in the Lutheran Church of Australia.

I happened to be staying at the seminary in Adelaide as a university student at the time. I'd just been out playing casual volleyball after tea and gone up to my room to begin studying, when I suddenly fell down face-first onto the floor. I couldn't move a muscle! This voice then spoke, as clearly as if someone was lying beside me. It simply said, "I want you to become a pastor." It came out of nowhere. I hadn't been thinking of becoming a pastor, and no one had ever suggested it to me. To clarify, it was not that I was against the idea–it's just that I'd never even considered it.

I remember saying, "Um ... okay!" (What else do you say when God has just pinned you to the ground after hitting you with a two by four?!!).

I actually then tested the call, just to make sure it wasn't me trying to get out of uni or something. I set myself to complete my science and education degrees and go teaching for three years, thinking that if the call was still there after that, I'd go back to study at the seminary. And that's what happened. The call was still there and back I went to study.

The amazing thing is that having had the call in that way it has sustained me through my studies and ministry when I have felt little confidence in my ability to be a pastor, and also once when I felt a strong, oppressive 'cloud' over me urging me to throw it in just before I graduated. It is like God knew what was coming and equipped me to deal with it well beforehand.

A number of years later, the truth of Psalm 91:11-12 dawned on me: about how angels are about to guard us in all our ways; lifting us up in their hands so that we don't strike our feet against a stone. I should have broken my nose or been hurt in other ways when I had fallen face down on the floor that day … but I was not hurt in any way at all.

The Returning Cows

Hollie Joyce

My name is Hollie Joyce, and I was raised on a farm in rural South Australia. I grew up knowing the Lord in a Christian family with many experiences of seeing God at work in my life, but there was one occasion that really opened my eyes to the help he provides us with as we call on his name.

At the end of Year 12 I came home to work on the family farm during the busy harvest season, where I learnt to drive the front-end loader for my main task of handling and feeding the cattle. We had just bought a very rowdy head of 60 cattle and a few bulls that enjoyed getting out of whatever pen or paddock they were put in. To keep them contained, we positioned them in our feed-lot that has high fences (but was across the road from our neighbour's wheat crop paddock that had no fence at the time). Full of confidence in my new tractor skills, I didn't think I would have a problem feeding those crazy cattle while all the men were out harvesting the crops–and all was fine for about a week.

One particular morning, however, I was driving the hay into the pen when the cows found their way out the gate and all began charging for the neighbour's ripe wheat crop. In a flurry I shot up a quick SOS to the Lord and stopped the tractor to run after them, knowing that rounding up those cattle in a ripe wheat crop was going to be near impossible. In any case I ran into the paddock, right around to the other side of them, as they began eating the full heads of grain. I stood there and not knowing what else to do, began ordering them to get back into the pen in the name of Christ Jesus. At this their heads turned, and every single one of them ran straight back into the pen!!

I couldn't believe what I had seen and don't know exactly how it happened, but I know God was with me and if we call on him, he will help us through whatever situation we find ourselves in.

The Foot

Name withheld

I was learning to drive my boyfriend Paul's car. I was reversing, and the car was about to go over a steep bank into the Fitzroy River when I felt a foot press heavily on my foot on the brake pedal. It was not Paul's. This action saved both of our lives. I feel that either Paul or I were saved for some important future purpose that day.

The Unknown Woman

Name withheld

When my dad, Ken, was a boy, he had a bad case of gastroenteritis and his parents were afraid he was dying. A woman came into the house, laid her hands on Ken and said, "You will live." From that time Ken steadily got better. His parents both assumed that the woman was the other's relative, but, in fact, no one knew her.

The Gift of Extra Time

Margot Durow

Some years ago my husband had a serious accident. At this time, I was booked on a flight to Fiji, to spend a weekend away with my family to celebrate my niece's 50th birthday.

Immediately I told my husband I would not be going. This, however, made him so upset and agitated the medical specialist advised me to take the trip–saying it was only three days and my husband would be just fine. In the end I could only pray to God to give me an answer to this.

Two days before I was due to fly out, I was returning to the hospital from lunch when suddenly a voice in my head said, "Don't go to Fiji!" This was accompanied by the feeling of having a glass wall in front of me. I was aware of everything going on around me, but I was momentarily prevented from moving. It was the strangest feeling. I thank God every day for that message because one day after I was due to leave, my husband sadly passed away. I was so thankful I was able to spend those last hours with him.

The Healing of the Sheep

Andrew Vonow

Dad and I were out rounding up sheep today when we found one caught in the fence, its right back leg strung within the top wires. Its legs were stretched out, its body lying upside down on the ground. We looked at it in loss, knowing that if its leg was broken, or unusable, it wouldn't be able to lie there much longer. We unstrung its leg and laid it on its side, hoping it would be alright. However, all it did was lay there with its leg thrashing and thumping up and down in a limp, utterly helpless way.

Rather than giving up hope, and knowing that we have a mighty strong shepherd we thought could give us a hand–or in this instance, a healed leg, we knelt there on the ground and prayed for this sheep's leg. After we had prayed, we let the sheep lie there for a bit, and then, since it had stopped its thrashing, we picked up its body and allowed it strength on its legs. When we did this, it tried to kick away with its good legs but fell over again. Praying all the while, we tried again, and this time the sheep got up, and resting against Dad, started limping away. Dad let it go by itself, and it started walking! We let it go, and drove off to round up the other sheep. When we came back to it, as we neared the gate, it started trying to run after the other sheep. Its leg was still a little weak, but it was giving it a solid effort.

In summary, we found a sheep caught in the fence which was

just about ready to die, we set it free and prayed for it, and God healed its leg and gave it strength to run. Thank you, Lord! I honestly believe that if God is willing to give new life to a sheep, he is more than willing to give new life to us. Receive his love, energy and strength, and in you he will do great things.

> *Consider the ravens: they neither sow nor reap, they have neither storehouse nor barn, and yet God feeds them. Of how much more value are you than the birds!*
>
> Luke 12:24

The Strong Hand

Norelle Behrendorff

It was a Saturday afternoon, and I was driving home from Brisbane with my husband along the highway. A bad pain started building up in my lower back and I became quite uncomfortable. The only thing I could think of was how good it would be to be home having a strong coffee and some strong pain killers.

We were only about five minutes from home when we found ourselves in a most dangerous and unusual situation. Through my blurred vision I was able to detect that we were driving through trees. While this was happening, and I was trying to steer us back onto the road, I had felt a strong hand (not my husband's) holding me firmly in my seat.

When our four-wheel-drive had finally stopped, I was unsure of what had happened. The one thing I did know for sure, however, was that God's hand had protected me from serious injury. I was very shaken, and despite the fact that the ambulance had attended, didn't need to go to hospital. Neither did my husband. He was also protected from injury. Why, what, and how it really happened, we have never and probably will never know.

The vehicle was completely written off as I had actually driven through a forest of trees on the side of the road at 100 kilometres per hour. The windscreen was broken and glass was everywhere. When my husband went back that afternoon to check the area, he had found a few steel pegs sticking out of the ground where he assumed signs were to be erected. He figured that the car's tyres must have blown out when I ran over them.

Something I know for sure through this ordeal, is that our loving God's hand was placed firmly over my chest that day to hold me firm through what could have been a very serious accident. I will not forget it as long as I live. We will never know why some things happen to us in life, but I do believe that no matter what we do go through, he protects us, loves us, and keeps us close to him.

Blessings to each of you who read this article.

The White Dove

Margaret Ward

Recently I was looking in a bird book for a certain bird that had just appeared in our area–then I went through and saw pigeons and doves.

At this I recalled the time in Bible College in 1961 when my boyfriend and I were having a hard time emotionally. One day out of the blue, a beautiful white dove had come to stay in the college garden. To me she was God's word of peace in that place, and I felt in my own spirit that God would really work out my life for his glory. Each day I saw the dove she emphasised God's peace to me. For about three weeks she stayed and others were blessed with peace also.

I remember that my boyfriend wanted to kill the dove. He wanted his way rather than God's way.

An Italian couple was greatly blessed also, when the dove came into their room. The wife had previously been unable to conceive, but before long was able to, and had two wonderful sons. This couple and their family became missionaries in Corsica, Sardinia.

God has many ways to get his word and peace to us.

The Power on My Back

Edna Randall

My husband had to have a medical procedure in the Brisbane Hospital. In the morning at the motel, I prayed for him and the doctors, that he would be cared for and that I would cope whatever the result, and be protected.

He was admitted at 9am and discharged at 4pm. After being discharged he said he would like a nice take-away from the Breeze Cafe, and that he would wait for me outside.

I ordered the meal and paid for it, but as I stepped back, my heel got caught on something and I lost my balance. Trying to right myself, I quickly started stepping back with arms extended, trying to hold onto something. By this time, I was leaning back and all I could see was the ceiling, thinking, *Who is going to look after him if I hit the tiled floor?*

It was at that moment I felt a power on my back lifting me to the upright position. The woman behind the counter saw all of this happening. Her eyes were huge, and her mouth wide open. She stood there like a statue, staring at me. Then she said after an amount of time, "Weren't you lucky?"

Quietly I collected my belongings and went out to find my husband. Trying to recover, I told him what had happened, to which he replied, "That must have been God who helped you!"

What an experience!

The God of Miracles

Joselyn Khan

The Lord my God has been wonderful to me from the beginning until today. To choose a few from a myriad of miraculous events in my life is an honour and a tribute to how beautiful and gracious the Almighty is. I hope it will encourage you to see him as a caring Father and confidante.

When I was 7, my mother had an argument with the person who drove us to school every day. Because of this, she gave me money to get to school on my own. I knew it wasn't enough but she wasn't to be corrected, and I wasn't to miss school.

I asked my God to help me and boarded the first bus. The driver gave me wrong change–more than what I had before! The second bus driver gave me the wrong change too. I got dropped off in the town, and from there I had to walk through the sheltered town and through an open industrial area to get to school. It began pouring down rain as I approached the open industrial area. I asked God to stop the rain maybe ... but instead, a man called out to me, "What are you doing, silly girl? Are you going to walk into the rain?" He placed his umbrella over me and walked me to school. The rain stopped when he smiled goodbye. I ran towards my school and looked back at my Good Samaritan for one last wave but he had disappeared. I strained my eyes to find him but there was no one as far as I could see.

When I was 10, I was sick with a cold; I had a fever and a chesty cough. My nani (grandmother) came to look after me. I was watching TV in the evening and she said to me, "Would you like me to pray for you?" I nodded and felt happy to have such special attention. I listened to her prayer closely and agreed wholeheartedly with her words. She was grateful to God our Father for life and family, she praised him and thanked him for all her children and grandchildren, and she asked for his loving mercy and love to restore all my bones and all my muscles. At this, I had a big sweat and the fever left me. I received my energy back and got well immediately.

When I was 18, I was in Brisbane, Australia, with a 'temporary' residence visa and Griffith University had accepted me to study Biomedical Science. However, my fees were too expensive on my temporary status. I was told if I could change over to a 'permanent' residence visa, I could be a commonwealth supported student and the fees would be halved.

My mother spent a lot of months on the phone with the Immigration Department and couldn't give me any sense of direction. We had to meet a lot of conditions for earnings, work sponsorship, length of stay and so on. I prayed in my room and asked my God what to do. Should I start looking for employment? What field should I apply in? Should I still be hopeful and start preparing for university? I was 18 and clueless.

The Lord then spoke to my heart, "3rd of March, you will be a full-time student." I felt a great calm in my soul, I thanked the Lord for lighting my path, and nothing caused me any anxiety from that moment on.

The day I received my permanent residence was a Saturday at 11am. The Immigration Office was to close at 1pm. How we made it into the city, found parking and got our visas stamped in two hours was a miracle of its own. Every light was green, every lane was clear, the lady at the office called out, "Everyone who just needs stamps please come this way; everyone else please return on Monday." The Lord parted the Red Sea!

I walked into uni the following Monday and received my enrolment pack. It said "Congratulations!" It was dated the 3rd March, 2008.

Even now, the Lord continues to perform miracles in my life. He has saved me from the scars of my past and teaches me a new way. Though I am a foreigner far from home, the Lord my God has blessed me with a new church family and children of my own who bring me joy.

I sought the Lord and he answered me; he delivered me from all my fears. Those who look to him are radiant; their faces are never covered with shame. Those who fear him lack nothing. Your love, Lord, reaches to the heavens, your faithfulness to the skies! Your righteousness is like the highest mountains, your justice like the great deep! How priceless is your unfailing love, O God! For with you is the fountain of life; in your light we see light!

Psalms 34 & 36 NIV

The Aura

Edna Vonow

In September 2011, I was involved in a horrific accident in which I sustained severe head injuries when my car collided with a train at a level crossing. I was carried 50 metres down the track and my car was left an unrecognisable pile of metal. A friend later told me that during the 'jaws of life' rescue, an SES worker had seen an aura of light over me. I interpreted the light as being God's direct intervention on the scene. Over ten years later, and by the grace of God, I am still alive, having been given a second chance to live in his name.

While in the hospital, during the early stages after the accident, I had a vision of being in heaven with Jesus with him holding my hand. It was so beautiful. When I woke up, I was so disappointed that I was still here.

For me to live is Christ and to die is gain.

Philippians 1:21 NIV

Jesus Loves Me

Merrelyn Zanker

This relates to the previous story.

My 75-year-old mother had just been in a car versus train accident, and had sustained very serious head injuries. My brother, Kingsley, and I were with her in the Accident & Emergency Department of our local hospital. Mum was very agitated, both verbally and physically, due to bleeding in her brain. We continually attempted to keep her still, encourage her to leave the neck brace on, and to lie down. We prayed with her, constantly reassured her, and quietly sang Christian songs and hymns to her. Virtually nothing helped. The doctors decided she needed to go the Royal Adelaide Hospital by air that night. We did not know what her future held. Mum was moved into another room to be prepared for the flight.

What happened next amazed us ... all at once she sang with the clearest voice, the entire first verse of 'Jesus Loves Me', with not a single mistake or note out of place. She then went completely calm–so calm, in fact, that I quickly glanced at my brother and then at the heart monitor to see if she was still with us. Thankfully she was, and this reassurance put me completely at ease. At that moment I knew that Mum did indeed have Jesus on her side–he was her all in all; he loved her. I believe Jesus was also reassuring us through Mum.

Nine days later the doctors in the Intensive Care Unit planned to remove her ventilator to 'see what her body wanted to do'. We all gathered as a family, prayed, had communion, sang 'Jesus Loves Me', and said our goodbyes in the knowledge she might not make it.

Contrary to the opinion of the neurosurgeon, Mum did stay with us–her first words being "Jesus loves me, Jesus loves me, Jesus loves me," over and over again as she emerged from her coma! We were all so incredibly moved by her faith and believe it confirmed how completely infused Jesus was in her life. I felt that if they were the last words we ever heard her speak, everything would be alright.

It is now more than ten years since the accident, and Mum is still here with us. When people say to her, "You're a miracle," she says, "No, God's the miracle!"

I believe this story shows the direct intervention of God. It attests to the love of God for us, his protection of Mum, and how our mother's love for Jesus, and mostly his love for her shines through.

Common Themes

If one takes these stories as a whole, various common themes emerge:

The angels that are seen and/or felt, are most often dressed in white, are male or have indistinct features, carry out their assigned duty and then disappear, bring a message of hope or guidance (or have rescued/protected in some way), they are usually accompanied by a feeling of great peace, their timing is always perfect, and they always appear at times of greatest need.

Regarding the visions–when people see their loved ones in heaven, it always fills them with an overwhelming sense of assurance, joy and comfort, the details are extremely vivid, and their loved ones most often appear in white and are fully alive; 'the door' is a recurring theme–finding the door, not being able to find the door, not the right time to go through the door; and many occur at low or difficult times in people's lives. Visions of Jesus tend to supercede all else.

When voices are heard, they always come at strategic times and bring direction and/or comfort. Often they come at night (as perhaps this is when it is quiet, our minds are not so cluttered, and we can easily distinguish these voices from everyday chatter).

Whenever people relayed their story (which, incidentally, was often triggered by a traumatic event) to me, whatever it was, it was as though it just happened. The recall of detail was unprecedented. I believe there is something remarkable about a 'God' experience that sets it apart from all others.

Mary C. Neal in her book, *To Heaven and Back* says,

> *"The human brain is quite good at remembering events, but not usually so adept at remembering the precise details. If you ask most people to describe their wedding, a child's birth, or other such important events, the tiny details will have faded and the stories will likely have changed some over time ... even vivid dreams rarely stay in our memories for more than a few minutes.*
>
> *I have observed one of the truly remarkable and consistent aspects of accounts of experiences that involve the presence or intervention of God is that the description of the experience remains constant no matter how much time has elapsed. People who have been involved in a Godly experience remember with clarity and constancy the details of the incident and vividly recall their emotions as though they had just occurred."* [4]

May the glimpses of God's love as shown in this book whet your appetite for more of God and what he has for you!

For from him and through him and to him are all things.
To him be the glory forever. Amen

Romans 11:36

Bibliography

1. www.ChristianAnswers.Net (Dr Paul Eymann and Dr John Bechtle).
2. Angels–A Bible Study, by Linda Stover http://www.hoshuha.com/articles/angels.html
3. Neal MD, Mary C., To Heaven And Back, Waterbrook Press: Colorado Springs, 2011 p 99.
4. Neal MD, Mary C., To Heaven And Back, Waterbrook Press: Colorado Springs, 2011 pp 137,138.

www.ingramcontent.com/pod-product-compliance
Lightning Source LLC
Chambersburg PA
CBHW050311010526
44107CB00055B/2200